# THE UNKNOWN
# JESUS

## PERCEPTION VS. REALITY

## What the Historical Record Tells Us

Edited by **BOB GUCCIONE, JR.**

**CENTENNIAL** BOOKS

# THE UNKNOWN
# JESUS

## PERCEPTION *vs.* REALITY

### What the Historical Record Tells Us

# CONTENTS

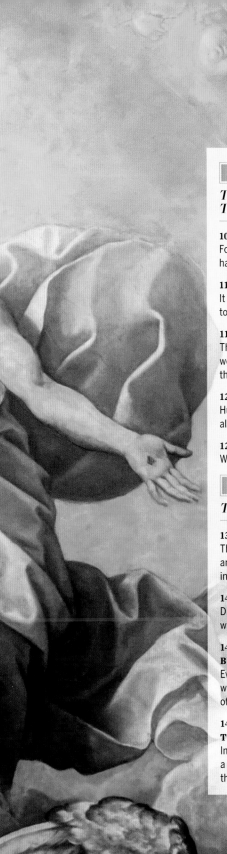

# WHO WAS JESUS CHRIST?

HE HAS THE MOST RECOGNIZABLE NAME ON THE PLANET,
YET MUCH OF HIS TIME HERE ON EARTH IS STILL SHROUDED IN MYSTERY.

IN *THE UNKNOWN JESUS*, YOU'LL LEARN MORE ABOUT the most famous person in history—and someone whom we actually know staggeringly little about. He is believed to be God by over a third of the world's population, someone who walked the Earth for a scant 33 years as a human, and who died as a man but rose approximately 48 hours later as immortal and divine, having shed our mortality. Forty days after that, he ascended to heaven, to return, so to speak, to the family business.

Jesus Christ is the most recognizable person who ever lived, and yet we don't even know what he really looked like. There's probably no one, in any remote corner of the world, who can't identify him. But it's doubtful that Christ actually appeared as he has been portrayed in countless paintings, sculptures and other artwork. He surely wasn't tall, pale-skinned with flowing, auburn-colored hair and beard. More likely, he would have been short and darker like the other Jews of Judea and surrounding region at the time of his birth.

There's only one written record of his existence and movements, found in the Bible, which was authored decades after his death, by people who almost definitely didn't know him (one of the Gospel writers may have been John the Apostle but nobody is certain). It was then edited and massaged over the centuries to fit the chosen narrative of the religion he didn't found. (Jesus didn't even want to start a new religion—and never referred to himself as the Son of God—he only wanted to transform Judaism, and preached the previously unseen possibilities of the scriptures of the Torah.)

After his birth, mystically rendered and mythologically remembered, and one instance where his parents lose track of him and find him teaching in the temple at the age of 12, we know nothing of the first 30 years of Jesus' life. Where did he go, what did he do? Did he learn carpentry and work with his father, or did he travel the known world seeking deeper spiritual knowledge? There are flimsily supported theories that he traveled to Tibet and India to study their faiths. That, for a host of reasons, is unlikely. But no one knows—there's just darkness until the Bible picks up the story again, with gusto, with Jesus' baptism by John in the River Jordan and the beginning of his ministry.

And where is Jesus now? He's probably not sitting on a park bench in heaven, waiting for us to join him; he's more dynamic than that. The living, Cosmic Christ is, one would have to think, everywhere, all the time, and with us in ways we can't begin to understand. We hope this book will unravel some of the mystery and misperceptions. —*Bob Guccione, Jr.*

Jesus, who is frequently referred to as the Good Shepherd, is often portrayed holding a lamb, a symbol of his loving philosophy.

Though parts of Jerusalem predate even Jesus' time on Earth, its skyline has changed dramatically over the centuries.

CHAPTER

# 1

*Prepare the Way
of the Lord!*

# THE BIRTHPLACE OF JESUS

ANCIENT JUDEA, WHERE CHRIST WAS BORN, WAS A SLEEPY REGION UNTIL THE ROMANS CAME. THEY TURNED IT INTO A VIBRANT CORNER OF THEIR EMPIRE, WHICH, IN TURN, CREATED IMMENSE DISCORD AND SET THE STAGE FOR JESUS TO BE PERCEIVED AS THE MESSIAH WHO WOULD LIBERATE THE JEWS FROM THE ROMANS—WHICH IS NOT EXACTLY WHAT HE HAD IN MIND.

IN ORDER TO GET A GOOD UNDERSTANDING OF WHO Jesus was, it's important to set the scene: Most of the events in the Gospel take place in Judea, which included Jerusalem; Galilee, where Nazareth was located; and Samaria, which lay between the two. Around the era of Jesus' time on Earth (thought to be between around 4 B.C. to A.D. 36, not precisely A.D. 1 to A.D. 33, due to small mistakes with the Roman calendar), they evolved rapidly from a small agrarian region to a major source of the Roman Empire's wealth.

Before the Romans moved in, most of the economy in Samaria and Judea was agriculturally based, producing grains, olives, grapes and figs and raising livestock. Judea probably had no more than 14,000 inhabitants. Galilee was similarly agrarian, but the Sea of Galilee was rich with fish and gave residents another opportunity to feed themselves and to trade. The majority of the population were tenant farmers who worked the land for royalty or other landowners. There was also a small class of wealthy aristocrats or merchants who dealt with coastal cities on the other side of the Mediterranean. They could afford servants or slaves to work the land and apparently spent their free time in spiritual pursuits.

But for the people outside of those fortunate few, life was mostly dedicated to the daily struggle of feeding themselves and their families. Constantly toiling, facing high infant mortality and a low average life expectancy, the people in Judea, Samaria and Galilee formed tight tribal bonds that usually superseded any loyalties to a state or government. These tribes were composed of several families, including distant relatives, who lived together in compounds of separate houses with a shared courtyard. The homes of the wealthier people were built with fitted, square bricks of clay that offered superior protection from the elements.

The lower classes occupied huts made from stones that were rougher and oblong. They patched gaps with a combination of clay and grasses, but these dwellings provided poor shelter.

Families were led by a patriarch, who was responsible for administrative decisions but also worked the fields, tended livestock or went fishing with other male members of the family or any slaves that the family could afford. Texts from this time focused almost exclusively on men—women's roles were mostly ignored, but women did play a key role in the tribal unit. In addition to being the primary

In the foreground are the ruins of Susita, a Roman town; beyond them is the Sea of Galilee.

caretakers and nurturers of the children, they spent a large portion of their day preparing food and were the social nexus for the community, including recommending spouses for their children.

Jesus was most likely raised in a small but growing middle class made up of artisans like clay workers and (in Jesus' presumed case) carpenters. These families provided essential services for the community, so they had a good amount of administrative sway. It is generally believed that Joseph, Jesus' earthly father, owned a carpentry business that was most likely very profitable in the small, 300-person village of Nazareth. This success would have allowed Joseph to travel to larger cities close by and to provide his children with an education in Jewish Scripture.

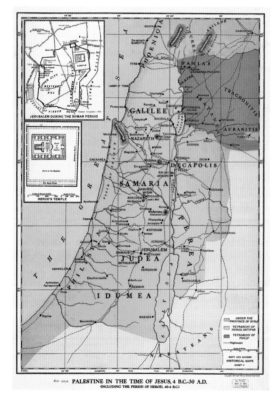

This map shows Judea, Galilee and neighboring regions in Jesus' time. "The Great Sea," which it undoubtedly was to the Jews of 2,000 years ago, is the Mediterranean.

Shortly before Jesus was born, the area came under the control of the Roman Empire. When the Romans occupied Judea and surrounding regions around 63 B.C., they left the Hasmonean dynasty (which had ruled with an iron fist since 140 B.C.) in charge. But the Hasmonean King Antigonus was overthrown in a brutal three-year war against Herod the Great that ended in 34 B.C., making Herod a client king.

The early relationship between the Romans and Jews was cordial and largely bureaucratic. Imperial Rome collected taxes and maintained control of the important trading routes, but left most of the local, day-to-day administration up to Herod and his bureaucrats. Troops could be called upon to protect the area from outside forces, but they were never garrisoned there. Still, their influence was unavoidable, and the result was that tensions that would occasionally boil over.

With the backing of Rome, Herod threw himself into public works projects all around the Kingdom of Judea. His efforts turned Jerusalem into a pilgrimage destination, with a grand temple. Herod created jobs and further integrated the region into the Mediterranean economy and eventually expanded into Galilee and Samaria. But this cost money, which meant increasing levies on landowners and farmers.

On top of his steep taxing, Herod was known to be a tyrant. He most likely used secret police to quell any discontent, and he paraded around the region with a bodyguard of 2,000 soldiers. Although he attempted to follow traditional Jewish rules, he also made many insensitive moves by introducing foreign forms of entertainment and replacing the high priests.

Although it is most likely *not* historically accurate, in the New Testament according to Matthew, Herod ordered all boys under the age of 2 in Bethlehem to be killed, after the Three Wise Men told him they were looking for the newborn baby who would be the king of the Jews. (Ironically, it was his son Herod Antipas who would condemn Jesus to death.)

Galilee was very much on the periphery of Herod the Great's vision, but it began to transform under Herod Antipas. When Antipas took control of Galilee, he began work on multiple public projects, bringing

*Mount Gerizim is sacred to the Samaritans, who view it as God's chosen spot for his Holy Temple.*

about rapid economic changes. Until that time, Galilee, which surrounded the Sea of Galilee (actually the lowest freshwater lake in the world), was a sparsely populated area where people lived off of fishing and farming the fertile land. But under Antipas, Sepphoris, the city closest to Jesus' home, became a center for trade, with heavy Roman and Greek influences.

Like his father, Antipas taxed people heavily. And, unsurprisingly, there was a lot of fraud perpetrated by Antipas' collectors. One day while preaching, Jesus was asked by followers of Herod, hoping to trick him into taking a side, whether it was lawful to pay taxes to the Emperor. Jesus responded: "Render unto Caesar the things that are Caesar's, and to God the things that are God's." (Mark 12:17) The passage ends: "And they marveled at him."

South of Galilee, Samaria was also undergoing urbanization and modernization of its economy. The capital of Samaria was also called Samaria but Herod changed it to Sebastus and transformed it into a tribute to the Greco-Roman lifestyle. He built high walls, a giant acropolis, a stadium and a grand Roman temple dedicated to Augustus.

Samaritans were somewhat unique among the Jews in Galilee and Judea. They had a separate temple on Mount Gerizim that they believed was the original Holy Place. Although culturally, they were very similar to the Jews of Galilee, the Samaritans traced their lineage back to the tribes of Joseph, Ephraim and Manasseh, and looked down on the Galileans.

As a result, there was animosity between the Jews from Galilee and those from Samaria. This is the context for Jesus' allegory of the Good Samaritan in which a Samaritan, despite cultural differences with a Jew whom he finds injured on the road, helps him to an inn and pays for his stay. Nevertheless, the relationship between the two groups was marred by crises in which the Galilean Jews destroyed the Samaritan temple; then two centuries later—because revenge is a dish best served cold—the Samaritans desecrated a Jewish temple with human bones.

One by one, Judea, Samaria and Galilee were wrested from control of the Herod family by the Romans in the early first century. Unrest between the Jews and Romans grew more frequent and came to a head in what is known as The Great Revolt, and The First Jewish-Roman War, in A.D. 66.

It is within this time span that Jesus' movement found its historic, ultimately world-changing footing. Even though he wasn't the liberator they had been hoping for, Jesus was able to appeal to Jews disillusioned with Herod and the Romans. These proved to be the perfect conditions to welcome a new prophet. ◆

Countless artists
have striven to
portray Mary as
she might have
truly appeared.

The Virgin Mary
By Francesco
Raibolini
ca. 1505

# THE STORY OF MARY

FROM HER FIRST YEARS WITH HER PARENTS,
ANNE AND JOACHIM, TO HER DAYS AT THE TEMPLE OF JERUSALEM,
THE VIRGIN MARY'S CHILDHOOD WAS FILLED WITH JOY.

MARY, MOTHER OF GOD; THE BLESSED VIRGIN; THE Virgin Mary. No matter what name you use—and there are hundreds worldwide—the fact remains that Mary is the most famous mother in the world. *National Geographic* took it one step further. In a 2015 cover story, they called the Virgin Mary "the world's most powerful woman." Little is known of Mary from Scripture; she speaks only four times in the New Testament. But her impact has reached every corner of the globe. Christians and Muslims revere her, frequently seek her intercession, and view her as the ultimate maternal figure. Some believe she is almost as important as Jesus himself. This is her story.

The first mention of the Virgin Mary in the Bible, at least by name, is in the Gospel of Luke, when she is being greeted by the Angel Gabriel: "Hail thee! Blessed art thou among women!" (Luke 1:28) The angel then goes on to deliver astounding news: This young virgin will soon conceive a child—without sin—who is the son of God!

Mary is actually prophesied at least two times in the Old Testament. In Genesis 3:15, God is addressing the serpent (aka the Devil) in the Garden of Eden: "I will put enmity between you and the woman, and between your seed and her seed; he shall bruise your head, and you shall bruise his heel." Many believe this means that the Virgin birth will ultimately kill off the Devil. The message in the Book of Isaiah is more clear:

> *"Behold, a virgin shall conceive, and bear a son, and shall call his name Immanuel."*

## "HAIL MARY, FULL OF GRACE, THE LORD IS WITH THEE! BLESSED ART THOU AMONG WOMEN!"
*—Luke 1:28*

### ANNE AND JOACHIM
The Bible reveals nothing about Mary's early life; but tradition and apocryphal writings, noncanonical works written in the style of scripture, help fill in the blanks. The parents of Mary are widely believed to be Joachim and Anne, a wealthy couple who first lived in Galilee and then settled in

*The Nativity
of the Virgin Mary*
By Ambrosius Benson
ca. 1528

Jerusalem, where the Virgin Mary was born and raised. The pair had been married for at least 20 years but remained childless, despite their prayers and promises to dedicate their firstborn to the service of God. In despair, Joachim retreated to the desert where he spent 40 days and nights. During this time, an angel appeared to Anne and told her, "thou shalt conceive and give birth and the fruit of thy womb shall be blessed by all the world." Joachim soon also received the same message from the angel and the couple reunited at the Golden Gate to celebrate the good news. Anne ultimately gave birth to a daughter, who was conceived without sin; they named her Miriam (Mary).

### TO THE TEMPLE

When Mary was 3 years old, her parents presented her to the service of the Lord at the Temple of the Virgins in Jerusalem. Catholic and Jewish traditions hold that this "virgin group" assisted the priests by performing chores, particularly sewing and cleaning; they also practiced worship. In an account from Anne Catherine Emmerich, the German nun and mystic who was renowned for her detailed visions of the life of the Holy Family, she described seeing the Virgin Mary during an episode of religious ecstasy. Mary was "being instructed in her prayers, as the priests were soon to come to examine the child in preparation for her reception in the temple. A feast

in preparation for this event is taking place in Anne's house, and guests are gathering there—relations, men, women and children.

"There are also three priests...who have come partly to examine the child Mary to see whether she is fitted for dedication to the temple, and partly to give directions about her clothing, which has to comply with a prescribed ecclesiastical pattern."

Of the day that Mary was taken to the temple, Emmerich wrote: "Mary had to ask the teachers and

## *THERE IS NO MENTION OF A MARRIAGE CELEBRATION FOR JOSEPH AND MARY IN SCRIPTURE.*

each of the young girls whether they would suffer her to be among them. This was the custom. Then they had a meal, and afterwards they danced amongst themselves." As part of the ceremony, "the priest cut off a few of her hairs and burnt them in a brazier."

By all accounts, Mary was blissfully happy during her years at the temple. She was "ever progressing in learning, prayer and work," wrote Emmerich. "She worked, wove and knitted narrow strips of stuff on

## { BIRTHPLACE OF MARY }

The Church of St. Anne in the old city of Jerusalem marks the site where many believe Joachim and Anne lived—and where the Virgin Mary was born. A previous church, built around A.D. 450 on this spot, was also dedicated to the Mother of God. With its austere stone exterior, the current church, which dates back to the 12th century, is a good example of medieval architecture. It is known for its remarkable acoustics, particularly well-suited for Gregorian chants.

long rods for the service of the temple. She washed the cloths and cleansed the pots and pans. I often saw her in prayer and meditation."

Mary stayed at the temple until age 12 or 14, when she was betrothed to Joseph.

### MARY, THE MOTHER OF JESUS

Roman Catholics hold firm to the following four dogmas regarding the Virgin Mary: The Immaculate Conception (many get this one wrong; this is the belief that Mary was conceived without sin—not Jesus). The Divine Motherhood (this one speaks for itself: Mary is the mother of God). The Perpetual Virginity of Mary (the notion that Mary remained a virgin her entire life). And finally, the Assumption of Mary into Heaven (the belief that Mary was taken up—body and soul—into heaven after her death).

Mainline Protestants, including Baptists and Presbyterians, agree with their Catholic counterparts on only one of these points: Mary is clearly the Mother of God. They do acknowledge the divine nature of the conception of Jesus, and they concur that Mary was a virgin at the time of his birth. But after that, most mainline Protestants take a different line—viewing Mary as an honorable woman, but certainly not sinless and likely not an eternal virgin, either.

In fact, in the 18th and 19th centuries, some Protestant denominations took a firm stand against what they considered to be the excessive veneration of Mary. They coined the term Mariolatry, which highlighted their belief that Catholics' obsession with Mary not only distracted from their worship of God, but actually bordered on idolatry. Catholics disagree. Yes, they venerate Mary, but they stop short of bestowing upon her divine adoration—that is reserved for God alone.

Even in modern times, this battle has sometimes become heated. In 2006, Catholics and Anglicans held a Marian festival at the Shrine of Our Lady of Walsingham in England. They were interrupted by a

*OF THE DAY THAT MARY WAS TAKEN TO THE TEMPLE, ANNE CATHERINE EMMERICH WROTE: "MARY HAD TO ASK THE TEACHERS AND EACH OF THE YOUNG GIRLS WHETHER THEY WOULD SUFFER HER TO BE AMONG THEM. THIS WAS THE CUSTOM. THEN THEY HAD A MEAL, AND AFTERWARDS THEY DANCED AMONGST THEMSELVES."*

*The Virgin With
Saints Anne and Joachim*
By Peter Ayres
1840

Left: *Presentation of the Blessed
Virgin Mary in the Temple*
By Juan de Borgoña
Date unknown

This panel captures the Annunciation: when the Angel Gabriel informs Mary that she will become the Mother of Jesus.

vocal crew of Protestants who showed up with signs that condemned "this idolatry."

## CHRISTIAN SCHISMS

The multiple churches that form the Anglican movement, which includes the Church of England and the Episcopal Church in the U.S., have widely varying views on Marian veneration. The high church—which sports many of the bells and whistles that are common in Roman Catholicism—has actually been sponsoring official pilgrimages to the Catholic stronghold of Our Lady of Lourdes in France since 1963.

Martin Luther, the founder of the Lutheran Church, flip-flopped throughout his life on how Mary should be viewed. As a young man he clearly revered

> ## "AND BEHOLD, YOU WILL CONCEIVE IN YOUR WOMB AND BEAR A SON, AND YOU SHALL CALL HIS NAME JESUS."
> —*Luke 1:31*

her and believed that she was both the Mother of God as well as a perpetual virgin. But he came to believe that God alone should be worshipped in this excessive fashion. Today, most Lutheran denominations admire Mary but don't honor her in any formal fashion.

John Wesley, the founder of the Methodist Movement, believed in Mary's perpetual virginity. Today the Methodist Church has no official stance on the Virgin Mary, other than following what is in scripture. In 2004, a small United Methodist Church in Chicago caused an uproar when the pastor brought in a statue of Our Lady of Guadalupe. Some Methodists fled. How could their church venerate the Virgin Mary? Neighboring Catholics were also disturbed. Still, the statue stayed, uniting all those who love the Virgin Mother. ◆

## { THE MUSLIM MARY }

Mary, the Mother of Jesus, is one of the most honored figures in Islamic theology. In fact, she is the only woman mentioned by name in the entire Koran. The Prophet Muhammad also listed her as one of the four greatest women of all time who had reached perfection. While Muslims believe in the virgin birth of Jesus, small details about his birth differ from accounts in the New Testament. Mary, known as Maryam, is a shining example for all Muslim women, who are known to visit both Muslim and Christian shrines, including the Bath of Mary in Jerusalem, where Muslims believe Mary once bathed. At this shrine, Islamic women pray for deliverance from infertility.

A Persian miniature portrait of Mary and Jesus, artist and date unknown

*St. Joseph With
Infant Christ*
By Guido Reni
ca. 1635

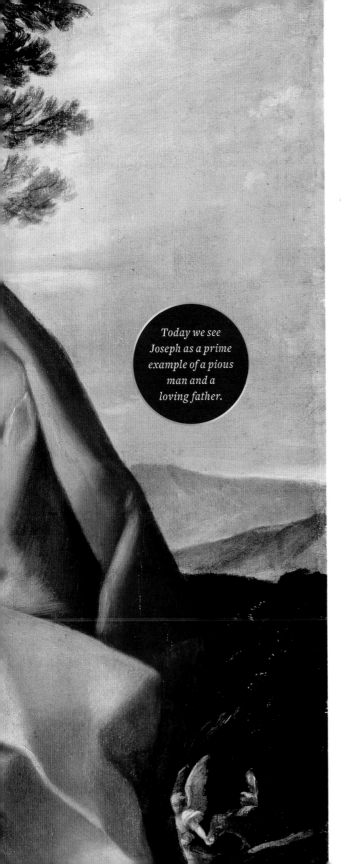

*Today we see Joseph as a prime example of a pious man and a loving father.*

# HIS EARLY YEARS

JOSEPH WAS A HAPPY, HUMBLE—
AND DEVOUT—CHILD WHILE
GROWING UP IN A LARGE
FAMILY IN BETHLEHEM.

**ST. JOSEPH, THE HUSBAND OF THE VIRGIN MARY AND** the foster father of Jesus Christ. What can we learn from his life? Although concrete details are few and his appearance in the Bible is limited to a few paragraphs in the New Testament, today we see Joseph as a prime example of a pious man and a loving father. God could have chosen a rich or powerful man to be the earthly caretaker of his son; instead, he opted for a humble carpenter. Joseph dealt with inexplicable events (such as his wife's pregnancy) with steadfast dignity. Most of all, he believed that doing God's will was paramount to all other concerns. Strength, humility and grace: Joseph symbolizes these qualities for 21st-century Christians.

Very little is known about St. Joseph's life. After his betrothal to Mary, only two New Testament evangelists, Matthew and Luke, include information about him. But a number of apocryphal works offer a possible glimpse of the early life of Jesus' earthly father.

*St. Joseph*
By Giovanni Francesco Barbieri
(called Il Guercino)
ca. 17th century

Right: *The Dream of St. Joseph*
By Philippe de Champaigne
ca. 1636

# { DREAM-FILLED DESTINY }

St. Joseph certainly did his fair share of listening to God—particularly in his dreams. Scripture outlines four distinct divine visits from angels, all from the Book of Matthew. In the first one, Joseph is informed to "not be afraid to take Mary as your wife." In the second dream, he is instructed to take Mary and baby Jesus and flee to Egypt to escape from the evil King Herod. In the third dream, he is given the all clear to return to Israel: "Go to the land of Israel, for those who were trying to take the child's life are dead." The final vision warns Joseph not to take his family to Judea.

In written transcripts of her visions, the venerable German nun and mystic Anne Catherine Emmerich details Joseph's childhood in Bethlehem as follows: "Joseph, whose father was called Jacob, was the third of six brothers. His parents lived in a large house outside Bethlehem, once the ancestral home of David, whose father Isai or Jesse had owned it."

Emmerich describes the 8-year-old Joseph as "very different in character from his brothers. He was very gifted and was a very good scholar, but he was simple, quiet and not at all ambitious. His brothers knocked him about and played all kinds of tricks on him."

As an adolescent, Emmerich recounts how Joseph sought to escape his brothers' constant teasing by visiting caves that were located on the other side of Bethlehem, "one of which was afterward the birthplace of Our Lord. He prayed there quite alone." Occasionally he sat with an elderly carpenter who

> ## "DO NOT BE AFRAID TO TAKE MARY HOME AS YOUR WIFE BECAUSE WHAT IS CONCEIVED IN HER IS FROM THE HOLY SPIRIT."
> —*Matthew 1:20–21*

"helped him with his work and so little by little [he] learnt his craft…. His master was a poor man, and made mostly only such common things…. Joseph was very devout, good and simple-minded, everybody loved him. I saw him helping his master very humbly in all sorts of ways—picking up shavings, collecting wood, and carrying it back on his shoulders. In later days he passed by here with the Blessed Virgin on one of their journeys, and I think he visited his former workshop with her." As an adult, Joseph is believed to have been employed as a carpenter: In the Gospel of Matthew, Jesus is referred to as "the carpenter's son."

*WE MAY NEVER KNOW THE EXACT DETAILS OF JOSEPH'S UPBRINGING AND LATER LIFE. THE PICTURE OF HIM THAT EMERGES FROM THE GOSPELS AND OTHER SOURCES, HOWEVER, DEPICTS AN EARNEST MAN, UNFAILINGLY DEVOTED TO HIS FAMILY— AND UNQUESTIONINGLY DEVOTED TO GOD.*

## ANGELIC INTERVENTION

When Joseph was 33, Emmerich says, an angel came to him, and he "received the call to betake himself to Jerusalem to become by divine decree the spouse of the Blessed Virgin." Matthew also describes this visitation in his texts: "An angel of the Lord appeared to him in a dream and said, 'Joseph, son of David, do not be afraid to take Mary home as your wife, because what is conceived in her is from the Holy Spirit. She will give birth to a son, and you are to give him the name Jesus, because he will save his people from their sins." (Matthew 1:20–25) This was the first of four dreams, all of which are described by Matthew. In the others, God later sends an angel to give Joseph warnings of impending danger that may bring harm to him and his family.

One question that remains to this date is what else might be said about Joseph's life before Jesus was born. Several times in the New Testament, mention is made of Jesus' "brothers and sisters" or "brethren." Is it possible that Joseph had been married before his betrothal to Mary? Written about A.D. 150, the Protoevangelium of James, which expands backward in time the stories in the Gospels of Matthew and Luke, suggests that Joseph was actually much older than Mary and had been married previously; these "brothers and sisters" were his children from this first union. Other apocryphal writings name this first wife as either Salome or Melcha and say that she and Joseph had six children together. The fifth-century writer and priest St. Jerome argued against this, saying that "we understand the brethren of the Lord not as sons of Joseph but [as] the cousins of the Savior, the sons of Mary of Clopas, his mother's sister." Mary of Clopas is mentioned in John 19:25 as being at the foot of the Cross with Mary.

We may never know the exact details of Joseph's upbringing and later life. The picture of him that emerges from the Gospels and other sources, however, depicts an earnest man, unfailingly committed to his family—and one who was unquestioningly devoted to God. ◆

St. Joseph the Carpenter,
the right panel of the
*Annunciation Triptych*
Workshop of Robert Campin
ca. 1427–32

Left: *Portrait of St. Joseph*
By Guido Reni
ca. 1635

*Mary travels to visit Elizabeth, while wondering how her betrothed husband will respond to the news of her pregnancy.*

Medieval Hungarian altarpiece, artist and date unknown

# WAS MARY A VIRGIN?

## CHRISTIANITY INTERPRETS MARY'S VIRGINITY AS A STATE OF PERPETUAL PURITY—BUT ARE WE MEANT TO TAKE THIS LITERALLY?

*"Therefore the Lord Himself will give you a sign: Behold, the virgin shall conceive and bear a Son, and shall call His name Immanuel."* —Isaiah 7:14

WHILE THE NEW TESTAMENT LANGUAGE IS CLEAR that Mary was a virgin when Jesus was conceived, scholars debate the meaning of the Old Testament prophecy to this effect. The Hebrew word "almah" in Isaiah 7:14 may be properly translated either virgin or maiden. The evidence, however, favors virgin. First, the word almah is never used in the singular of an unmarried woman except in the sense of virgin. Second, the New Testament authors, scholars in their own right, understood Isaiah to be referring to a virgin, where the Greek term is unambiguous.

As to their marriage itself, Mary and Joseph's betrothal would have been by arrangement and with the consent of the bride. It is conceivable that Joseph negotiated for marriage directly with Mary's parents. This would include agreement on a bridal price, a sum that Joseph would pay to Mary's parents at some point before completing the marriage. As in most Jewish marriages of the time, a written covenant was established, a benediction was pronounced, wine was shared and the man and woman were regarded as legally married.

The groom would then return home for a year-long preparation. Any unfaithfulness during this betrothal was considered adultery, deserving of the harshest penalties of the law, including death by stoning.

The scenario that played out in Mary's mind would have been a far cry from what actually happened. If they had followed tradition, when the wedding day arrived, Joseph would have dressed in splendid clothing, gathered his friends, and journeyed to fetch her. The timing would be a surprise to the bride—usually at night—but she would be prepared.

Mary would wear a special dress and veil and be greeted by her husband. Joseph's groomsmen would carry her in a litter to her new home. Along the way, family and friends would sing traditional marriage songs as the procession passed by. Once at the groom's home, she would be brought to a private room to consummate the union. Friends would symbolically guard the door for a while. Then the groom's father would offer a blessing and the feasting would begin, which could last for up to a week.

While this was the vision Mary and Joseph imagined, God had different plans. There is no mention of a marriage celebration for Joseph and Mary in Scripture. However, since being betrothed, they were technically married. The minimum required to complete their marriage was for them to begin living as husband and wife. Scripture is clear that Joseph took Mary as his wife and raised Jesus as his own son.

"For me, the issue centers not on the mechanics of reproduction but rather the nature of Jesus," evangelical writer Philip Yancey told *The New York Times*. "In the Incarnation, God's own self came to Earth as a human. I wouldn't pretend to guess how divinity interacted with human DNA, but that's the mystery the Virgin Birth hints at." ◆

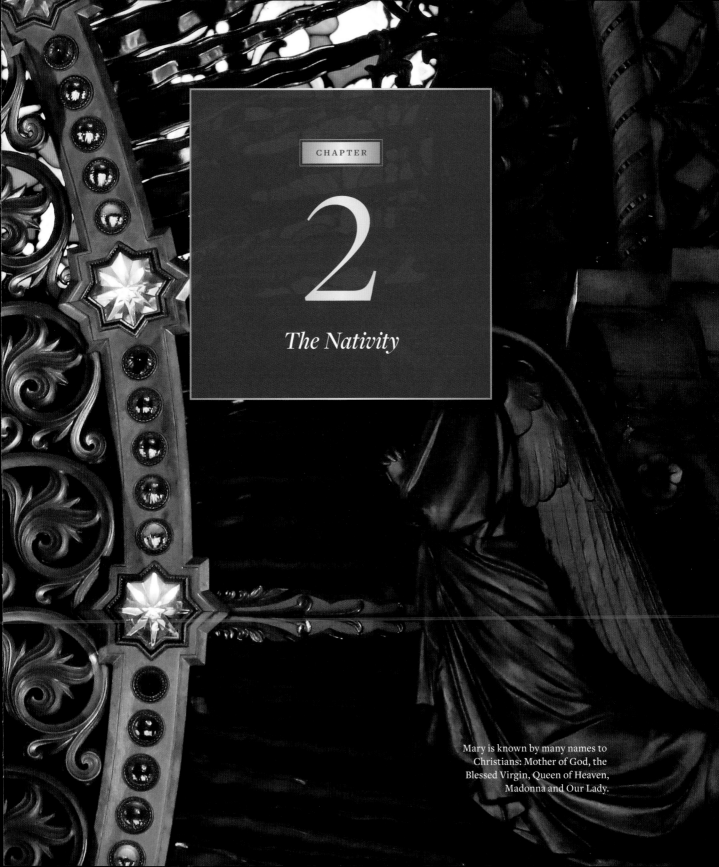

# 2

## The Nativity

Mary is known by many names to Christians: Mother of God, the Blessed Virgin, Queen of Heaven, Madonna and Our Lady.

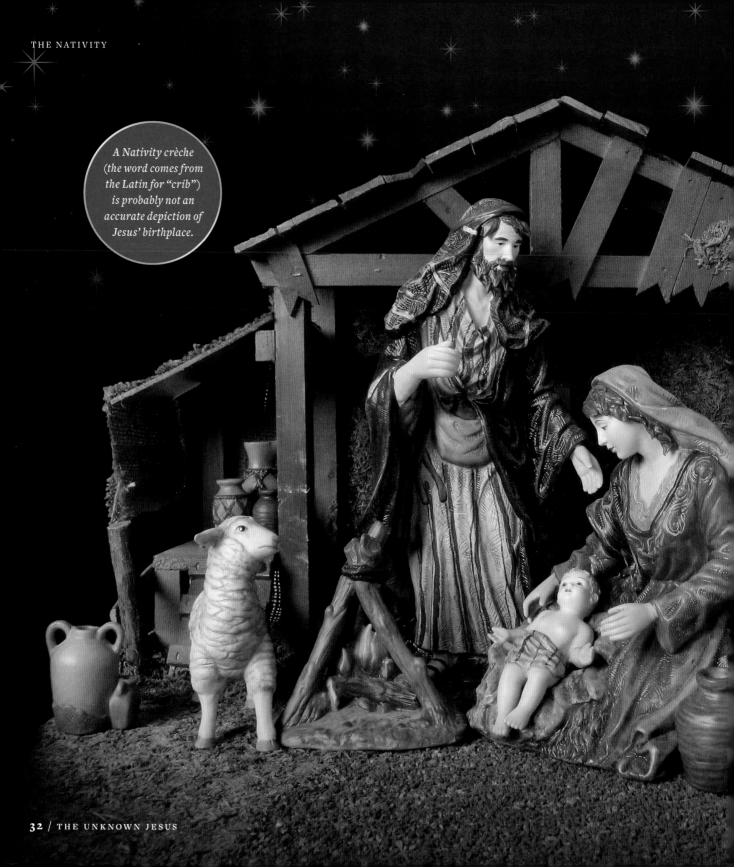

A Nativity crèche (the word comes from the Latin for "crib") is probably not an accurate depiction of Jesus' birthplace.

# THE CHRISTMAS STORY

WE THINK WE KNOW EVERYTHING
ABOUT CHRISTMAS, RIGHT?
BUT DO WE?

THE CHRISTMAS STORIES, OR THE INFANCY NARRA-tives as they are called in scriptural circles, are among the most beloved passages in the Bible. Nonetheless, they occupy a modest place, and are oddly different from the rest of the Gospel. How and why? There are two major reasons.

First, unlike most biographies, which begin with birth and end with death, with Jesus it is exactly the opposite: The "kerygma," or original preaching of the Gospel message as evident in the Acts of the Apostles, dealt with his death and Resurrection. Only much later did interest in Jesus' life grow. But by that time—three quarters of a century on—there was little historical material available. Thus, the first written Gospel, that of Mark, has no material on Jesus' origins at all; Matthew and Luke have differing versions, and the Gospel of John focuses exclusively on his divine origins.

The second explanation flows from this and is of critical importance: The Evangelists were manifestly more concerned with making theological points than writing pure history. Thus, in Luke, the first chapter is about comparing Annunciations, that to Zachary (father of John the Baptist) and that to Mary, the first encountering unbelief and the second belief. Nor do the traditions always agree. If Mary

Being born in a manger might not have been as controversial as it sounds, given the circumstances.

*The Nativity at Night*
By Guido Reni
1640

Right: *Adoration of the Shepherds*
By Federico Bencovich
ca. 1607–10

# { WAS JESUS BORN IN A MANGER? } Probably, yes! But not in a stable.

There has long been debate over whether Jesus was actually born in a meager manger—a makeshift crib—in a filthy barn, wrapped in swaddling clothes, surrounded by animals (and, visible or not, angels).

The controversy has mainly been, why would the Son of God be brought into this world in such desperate circumstances? Symbolism, maybe, but what does it really say or prove? That the humbly birthed Lord understood the commonest of humans? Surely that could have been just as easily established had he been born inside a house.

The reality is the manger—the trough horses and farm animals ate out of, not the stable, as is commonly mistaken when people think of the nativity scene— was a fine place to rest a newborn baby! As to the more disconcerting issue of why Mary went into labor outdoors, rather than inside, it is not simply, as the story goes, that the inn was full. More likely the family intended to stay with relatives, but there was no more room in the house, so they slept on the ground floor, under the living quarters, which was where the animals were kept at night. In the Middle Eastern climate, that would not have been a terrible hardship, if not exactly ideal accommodations.

So this probably wasn't some barn at the foot of someone's property, nor the result of people being insensitive to a heavily pregnant woman—which is the impression we are often left with in the nativity story.

It is widely believed that Jesus was born in Bethlehem, in Galilee, sometime between and 6 and 4 B.C. Most scholars refute Matthew and Luke's accounts that he was born in the Bethlehem of Judea (much farther from where Joseph and Mary lived in Nazareth), noting that these two Gospel writers wanted to establish a link for Joseph with the House of David, to be in line with Jewish belief that the Messiah would be born in David's city.

Hans Küng wrote in *On Being a Christian*: "It is admitted even by Catholic exegetes that these stories are a collection of largely uncertain, mutually contradictory, and strongly legendary and ultimately theologically motivated narratives, with a character of their own."

E.P. Sanders, ThD, a professor of exegesis at Oxford, also wonders about the authenticity of Luke's version, in which Joseph and Mary travel for a census taking place in Bethlehem, because they have been decreed to register in the town of Joseph's ancestor, David, who would have lived 42 generations ago. It would be impressive for Joseph, or anyone else, to trace their genealogy reliably back that far.

Matthew and Luke do identify a line of ancestors from Joseph that leads back to David. Even so, Sanders proposes that in that case, there would have been tens of thousands of descendants of David flocking to the tiny village of Bethlehem to register, flooding the system.

According to scholar John Dominic Crossan, ThD, the only mention of a census of Judea, Samaria and Idumea under Augustus was decades before Jesus' birth. Crossan also states that from Roman and Egypt taxation decrees, we can surmise citizens had to register where they lived and worked, not where their ancestors came from.

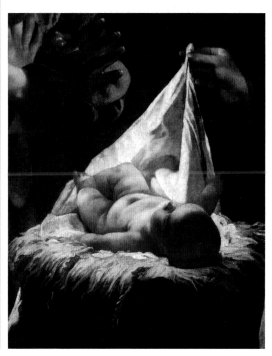

*Madonna Adoring the Christ Child*
By Antonio Allegri
(known as Correggio)
ca. 1524–26

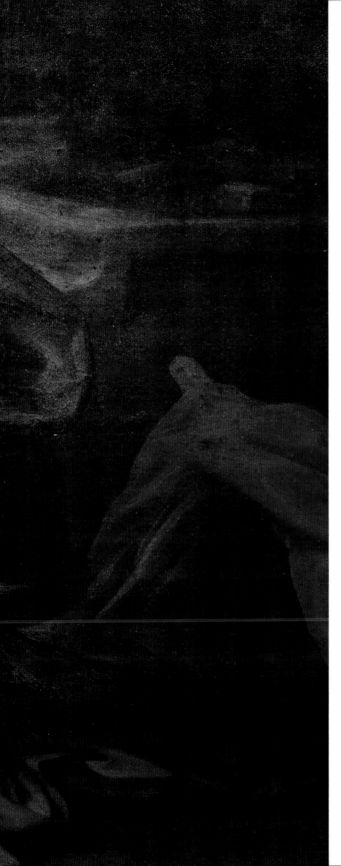

received such astounding, detailed information about the nature and person of the Son she was to conceive, why did she later say to the 12-year-old Jesus, "Your father and I" were seeking anxiously, and not at all grasp what He meant that he must be "in his Father's House"?

The most fascinating example, however, is Matthew. Written originally in Aramaic for Jewish converts, this Gospel presents itself as the new

> ## "WHILE CHRIST IS EVERYMAN, A WHITE, BLUE-EYED JESUS IS A DANGEROUS FICTION, AND NOT FACT."
> —*Father Michael K. Holleran*

Pentateuch or Torah, and Jesus as the New Moses. Its first word is "Genesis," and the genealogy it introduces does not at all correspond to the one in Luke, since the details are unimportant. The Flight Into Egypt is meant to correspond to Exodus and Hosea 11:1: "When Israel was a child, I loved him, and out of Egypt I have called my Son." The coming of the Magi and the slaughter of the infants by Herod correlate to the slaughter of the Hebrew firstborn sons by Pharaoh.

Many scholars no longer regard these stories as strictly historical. Yet, for revealing who Jesus is, and his significance, they are far more eloquent than a mere literal history would be. That is fact, and certainly no fiction! In addition, during the Sermon on the Mount, Jesus presents the Eight Beatitudes, which are far more challenging to observe than the Ten Commandments of Mount Sinai!

Finally: No one knows the day or month of Jesus' birth. As is well-known, December 25 was chosen to correspond to the winter solstice, symbol of the return of the Light, the coming of the true Son/Sun into the world. But the date of Jesus' actual birth is unknown. ◆

# HOW DID MARY AND JOSEPH GET TO BETHLEHEM?

TRAVEL WAS HARD, DANGEROUS AND SLOW. RATHER THAN RESORTING TO INNS, MANY PREFERRED THE HOSPITALITY OF OTHERS, ESPECIALLY KIN.

ACCORDING TO LUKE 1:3, A ROMAN CENSUS, ORDERED by Augustus Caesar, forced a pregnant Mary and Joseph to travel from Nazareth to Bethlehem, as all men had to register in their hometowns in order to be taxed by the Romans. As a descendent of King David, Joseph hailed from Bethlehem and still had family there. The trip was not an easy one: The couple traveled along well-established roads that were designed to connect the provinces to Rome, not to one another. This discouraged revolt, while allowing for goods to reach the capital city. Moreover, the system of Roman roads was largely undeveloped in Israel when Caesar Augustus called for a census. The roads traveled by Mary and Joseph would have been hard-packed dirt, winding through hilly terrain, with few places to stop along the way.

## TRANSPORTATION

The rate of travel depended on the mode of transportation. Travelers on foot could cover 16 to 20

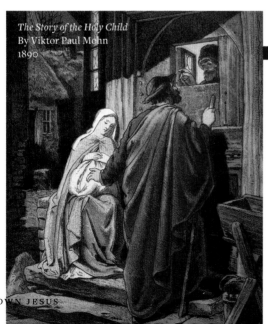

The Story of the Holy Child
By Viktor Paul Mohn
1890

## { INNS OF YORE }

Places of lodging sprang up along the main Roman roads. Owners were often well-to-do and leased their inns to a tenant landlord or left them under the management of slaves. These inns varied greatly in quality—most were dirty, many were used for drink and prostitution. Some were centers of crime. Innkeepers generally had a bad reputation. Inns were known for poor maintenance, leaky roofs, and uncomfortable sleeping arrangements. Most inns had stables attached to them. A simple meal was included in the price, though these varied in quality.

The situation improved in high-traffic areas, where multiple inns would have to compete for business.

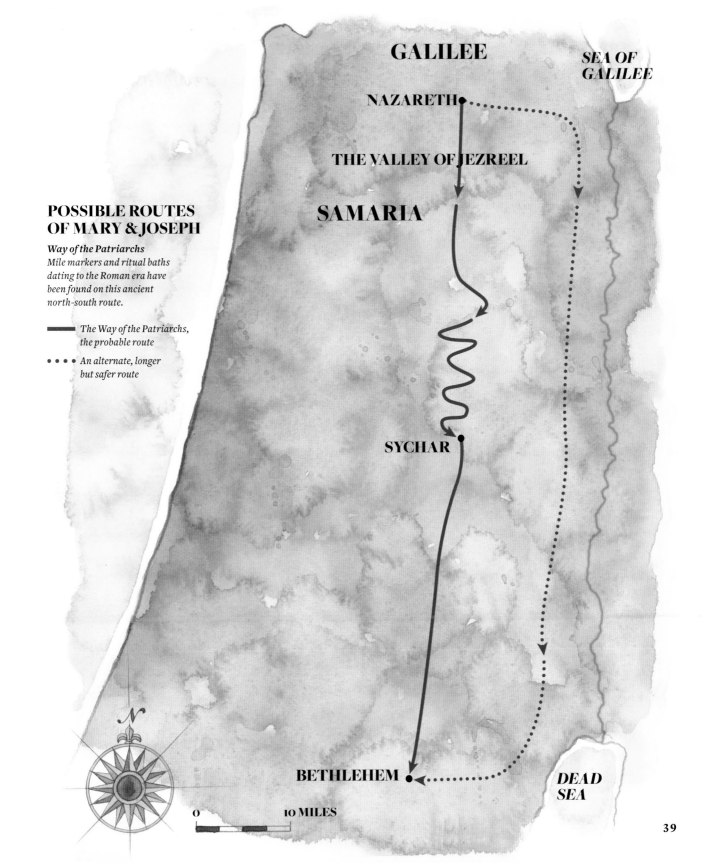

GALILEE

SEA OF GALILEE

NAZARETH

THE VALLEY OF JEZREEL

SAMARIA

## POSSIBLE ROUTES OF MARY & JOSEPH

**Way of the Patriarchs**
*Mile markers and ritual baths dating to the Roman era have been found on this ancient north-south route.*

——— *The Way of the Patriarchs, the probable route*

• • • • *An alternate, longer but safer route*

SYCHAR

BETHLEHEM

DEAD SEA

N

0    10 MILES

*After days of walking on unpaved, hilly trails, it would be a relief to finally reach the town of Bethlehem.*

*Joseph and Mary
Arrive at Bethlehem*
By William Brassey Hole
1906

miles a day. The wealthier, sometimes riding in carriages, might cover 25 miles per day—not a great improvement, as roads were often too crowded with pedestrians to go much faster. Couriers on horseback, generally in the service of the Roman Emperor, could cover as many as 50 miles in a day. There is evidence the wealthiest might travel in litters, carried by poles on the shoulders of slaves. Camels were common, as were oxen hitched to carts. Sure-footed donkeys were ridden by kings. Mary, being late in her pregnancy, might have traveled the 90 miles to Bethlehem at only 10 miles per day. She probably traveled on foot, not just because of the expense of a donkey, but because of the discomfort of riding one.

## THE ROUTE

Scholars are divided as to which route the couple followed. In one, the pair would bypass Samaria by heading east, south, and then back west. This would be longer, adding about two days to the journey. A second, more direct route, would head due south along a path called the Way of the Patriarchs. This is the more likely route. Even Jews who preferred to avoid Samaria used this route when large numbers of people would be traveling, such as for Passover or a census. The contemporary historian Josephus noted as much. The route was well-traveled, with well-known stops for rest and refreshment along the way.

It was also rich in Jewish history. Stretching back almost 2,000 years, Abraham, Isaac and Jacob would have walked these well-worn paths. Whether troops from invading nations or the armies of King David, every step covered by Mary and Joseph from Nazareth to Bethlehem would be, in a sense, the retelling of the history of Israel. Depending on Mary's stamina, the trip might have taken nine or 10 days.

## HOSPITALITY

Israelites considered hospitality a sacred duty. The value of hospitality was already ancient by Jesus' day. In arguably the oldest book of the Bible, Job defends his integrity, saying, "I have opened my doors to the traveler." This remained the expected norm. Travelers showed little compunction in asking for hospitality. The Old Testament book of 1 Kings records that when the prophet Elijah came to the town of Zarepheth, he asked a widow for a morsel of food and some water, despite her limited means. While the duty of hospitality was especially strong among family, it also crossed ethnic and national lines. Moses wrote in Deuteronomy, "Therefore love the stranger, for you were strangers in the land of Egypt."

A failure of hospitality was a punishable offense. Long after a breach of hospitality, the Law of Moses enjoined sanctions against Israel's neighbors. The Old Testament book of Deuteronomy states, "An Ammonite or Moabite shall not enter the assembly of the Lord…because they did not meet you with bread and water on the road when you came out of Egypt."

Hosts were duty-bound to protect their guests, accepting injury to themselves or their family rather than allowing a guest to be hurt. As an extreme example, Abraham's nephew Lot offered his daughters to the attackers to save his guests from harm, as they had already "come under the shadow of [his] roof" and therefore under his protection.

As a general rule, food was offered to guests who arrived before sunset. Those who arrived later were offered lodging only. When Mary and Joseph finally made it to Bethlehem, the problem was likely not a failure of hospitality but a lack of room. The population of Bethlehem had swelled. Homes were crowded. Every guest room was spoken for. Even so, customs of hospitality would have prevailed. It is unthinkable that anyone would have turned away Mary and Joseph, especially given her condition. The host would have figured out a way to make room. ◆

# { A POSSIBLE ITINERARY TO BETHLEHEM }

•**Day 1–2** Descent from the hills of Nazareth to the smooth plain of the Valley of Jezreel. This would have been the easiest part of Mary and Joseph's travels.
•**Day 3–4** Slow ascent out of the Jezreel Valley. Ancient olive groves still dot the landscape, some dating back to the first century.
•**Day 4–5** More challenging part of the journey. Switchbacks ascending and descending the mountains of central Israel. Each day would have ended at a well or spring, one of which could have been Jacob's Well in Sychar.
•**Day 6–7** Ever higher hills—the most uncomfortable part of the journey.

•**Day 8–9** First sight of Jerusalem off in the distance. Roads are more crowded. The temple dominates the horizon. Mary and Joseph arrive in Jerusalem.
•**Day 9–10** A few hours walk to Bethlehem, crossing hills and parched desert.

Yes, angels may have been looking on at the birth—but so, too, were oxen, donkeys and other livestock.

*Nativity With the Prophets Isaiah and Ezekiel* By Duccio di Buoninsegna ca. 1308–11

## {WHAT WAS MARY'S LABOR LIKE?}

Women gave birth either standing, squatting or sitting. They did not lie on their backs. In this manner, they did not have to push against gravity.

Archaeologists have unearthed Egyptian "birthing bricks." These bear the faint image of a woman giving birth, squatting with each foot on a brick. A midwife stands by, ready to catch the child. These may be the birth stools mentioned in Exodus, 14 centuries before Jesus. In the Roman world, there were special birthing chairs with a U-shaped hole in the seat and supports for the feet and back, and Jewish women would have used these. It is possible Mary may have used such a device.

An ancient relief shows how childbirth may have looked in Mary's time.

PERCEPTION vs. REALITY

# THE DATE OF JESUS' BIRTH

THE DATE OF THE NATIVITY HAS BEEN A SUBJECT OF SPECULATION
AND DEBATE. THE WRITERS OF SCRIPTURE OFFER FEW CLUES.

THERE IS NO MENTION OF ANY CELEBRATIONS OF the anniversary of Jesus' birth in the Bible. The Scriptures are silent on even the season of his birth. Some have offered a date based on the fact of shepherds keeping watch in the field by night, suggesting the lambing season in spring. Scholars are wary, however, of reading too much into such detail.

## PAGAN ROOTS?

A common supposition is Christmas was set on December 25 to coincide with pagan festivals such as the Roman Saturnalia or other major events. In A.D. 274, the Roman emperor Aurelian decreed a December 25 feast in honor of the birth of Sol Invictus, the Unconquered Sun. The theory suggests that early Christians conscripted this date to both redeem the date from pagan dominance and further the mission of evangelism. If pagans could convert their idolatrous feast days into celebrations of Christ, they might find it easier to convert their religion to Christianity.

This theory has its problems. The practice of Christianizing pagan rituals seems to have begun only after the conversion of the emperor Constantine, who reigned from 306 to 337. There is virtually no evidence prior to the third century of Christians adopting pagan practices or dates into their calendar. The December 25 date was already popular prior to this. And the earliest Christians did not speak of Christianizing the Saturnalia or other pagan festivals.

There is a more ancient theory of how December 25 was assigned as the date of Jesus' birth, based on the belief in Judaism that key events would happen that day. As early as A.D. 200, Tertullian calculated the date of the Crucifixion as March 25. Under the premise, unverifiable as it is, that Jesus was conceived and crucified on the same date, Tertullian concluded that he was born on December 25, nine months after conception.

A document from North Africa dated around the time of Constantine sets Jesus' birth at the time of the winter solstice, again calculating from the presumed date of his conception. Shortly thereafter, St. Augustine writes, "[Jesus] is believed to have been conceived on the 25th of March, upon which date he suffered. But he was born, according to tradition, upon December the 25th."

Eastern Orthodox churches used the same logic. They start at a different date of conception, April 6, and calculate January 6 for a birth date. Some Eastern churches still celebrate Christmas on January 6.

In any event, this assignment of a birth date was not based on the dates of pagan holidays or rituals, but on a belief that Jesus died on the same date on which he was conceived. While certain elements of modern Christmas celebrations may have been "redeemed" from pagan practices, it is difficult to highlight December 25 as the day—rather, it is most likely that the precise date of Jesus' birth has been lost in history. ◆

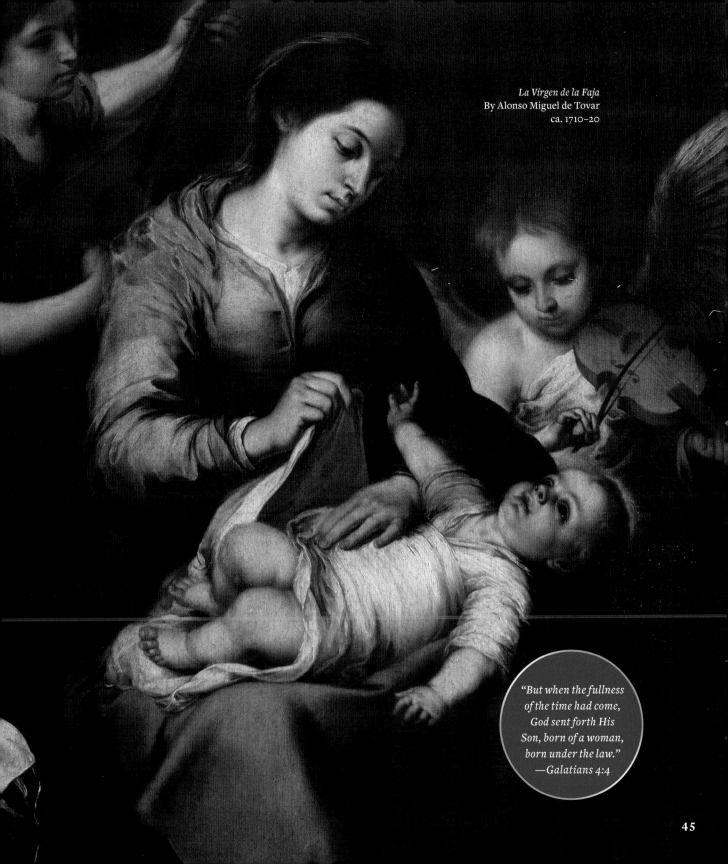

*La Virgen de la Faja*
By Alonso Miguel de Tovar
ca. 1710–20

"But when the fullness of the time had come, God sent forth His Son, born of a woman, born under the law."
—Galatians 4:4

45

Humble shepherds,
tending to their
flocks at night,
were the first to hear
of the divine birth.

*Annunciation to the Shepherds*
This fresco by Carlo Grimaldi
is from the 16th-century chapel
of Santa Maria dell Anima.

# ANGELS ANNOUNCE
# TO SHEPHERDS

AVERAGE PEOPLE DOING AVERAGE THINGS ARE UNEXPECTEDLY LIFTED
INTO EXTRAORDINARY MOMENTS WITH COSMIC RAMIFICATIONS.

WHEN THE ANGEL APPEARED TO THE SHEPHERDS, Luke says they were "out in the fields, keeping watch over their flocks by night." The angel did not appear to the chief priests or palace officials, but to a company of shepherds keeping watch beneath a starry sky.

Scripture offers no description of the heavenly interruption itself. Of the angel, we are told neither its shape, nor its appearance, nor how it marshaled for this moment. There is no description of the sounds it made or of the manner of its proclamation. But when the moment was right, the angel burst forth in a celebration fit for the birth of a king.

It was a spectacular sight. In the blackness of night, the appearance would have been blinding. A sudden flash. A breaching of the veil separating heaven and Earth. The shepherds quake with fear. They are dazzled and confused. The visitor is bright and beautiful and dreadful all at once. Who is it? What is it?

The angel encourages them, "Fear not!" The shepherds could barely look on. The shock of the angel's appearance formed a stark contrast with the pure happiness of its words. Good tidings. Great joy. All the people. The encounter was utterly overwhelming.

## { A FIELD WITH A HISTORY }

Among several locations claiming to be the site of the angels' announcing Jesus' birth is the town of Beit Sahur, also called the Village of the Shepherds, east of Bethlehem. As King David was born in Bethlehem, the fields here may be where young David tended his father's sheep. The burial location of Jacob's beloved wife Rachel is nearby. Further to the east is the Field of Ruth, where tradition says Ruth met Boaz. They married and she became the many times great-grandmother of King David. While the precise locations of most of these ancient sites cannot be verified, they serve as important reminders that these were real events happening to real people at real places.

# "AND BEHOLD, AN ANGEL OF THE LORD STOOD BEFORE THEM, AND THE GLORY OF THE LORD SHONE AROUND THEM, AND THEY WERE GREATLY AFRAID."

*—Luke: 2–9*

The angel delivers its breathtaking message: "For unto you is born this day in the city of David a Savior, which is Christ the Lord." The entire trajectory of human history had been aiming at this point. God promised the Messiah. Prophets predicted him. Centuries of rituals and multiplied thousands of sacrifices pointed to him. Priests taught him. God's people awaited him. Since the dawn of civilization, all earth had waited on tiptoe for the "seed of the woman" to come and crush evil at its source.

And now, in an unknown field, on an indeterminate date, to nameless, faceless shepherds, a glorious ambassador of heaven has winged its flight to Earth to announce the news. Christ is born! A Savior is given! Little else matters beside this.

The shepherds would recognize him, the angel said, by the sign of a baby wrapped in swaddling clothes, lying in a manger. Nothing had been by accident. The will of God had been perfectly achieved to the minutest detail.

### A HOST OF ANGELS

As if that were not enough, the visitation is suddenly multiplied. Celestial fireworks of majestic angels filled the sky, singing the gospel of God. "Glory to God in the highest, And on Earth, peace, goodwill toward men!" Luke calls them a multitude of the heavenly hosts, the armies of the living God. Their battle cry is of peace and good will—reconciliation between a world of fallen humankind and an utterly holy God, all centered in the baby in the manger.

As fast as they appeared, the angels were gone. The stunned shepherds gathered themselves.

Understanding the magnitude of the moment, they hurried to Bethlehem to see for themselves. There was Jesus, wrapped in swaddling clothes, lying in a manger and Mary with him. Like generations of people who would follow after, the astonished shepherds told everyone they could of the glories they had experienced and of the Savior they had seen. ◆

## { HEAVENLY HOST }

The vastness of angelic armies is beyond comprehension. They do the bidding of God, protecting his people and destroying his enemies. The obscure prophet Michaiah saw God on his throne, and all the host of heaven standing on his right and on his left. King David saw a detachment numbering in the thousands. When an army came to capture Elisha, he saw the mountain teeming with "horses and chariots of fire." They blinded the enemy and gave him victory. Daniel witnessed ten thousand times ten thousand—a number too great to count. They are an "innumerable company of angels." When the shepherds saw "a multitude of the heavenly host," the vision would have been utterly overwhelming.

*Mural of the Angel Gabriel Revealing*
*Christ's Birth to the Shepherds*
Artist and date unknown

Left: *Armed Band of Angels*
By Guariento di Arpo
ca. 1354

49

Camels can carry more
weight than horses
and need less water.

# FOLLOWING THE STAR
## WHAT DID THE MAGI SEE?

WAS IT A CELESTIAL BODY OR A SIGN FROM GOD THAT
BROUGHT THE WISE MEN TO BETHLEHEM?

THE STAR OF BETHLEHEM HAS BEEN A SOURCE OF wonder and debate for 2,000 years. Numerous theories have been proposed. Some say the Wise Men followed a comet. Another suggestion supposes an asteroid or fireball streaked across the Persian sky in the direction of Judea. Yet another theory suggests that God simply hung a miraculously bright star in the night sky over Bethlehem. But in all these instances, King Herod would have seen what was in the sky and more than the Wise Men would have visited Jesus.

Astronomers suggest that the Magi observed the gradual unfolding of an unparalleled celestial conjunction. Some have determined that shortly before the birth of Jesus, Jupiter, the King of the Planets, conjoined with Regulus, the King of the Stars, in the constellation of Virgo, the Virgin. To top it off, all this would have rested, from a vantage point in Persia, over Judea. The Magi could have correlated this phenomenon with the biblical prophecies of a Bethlehem-born son of a virgin. Whatever the Magi of Persia may have seen, they concluded a significant king had been born, worthy of not only a journey but also of the presentation of costly gifts.

## THEY CAME FROM THE EAST

Persia encompassed a large region centered over today's land of Iran. Over the centuries, the empire expanded and contracted. By the time of that first Christmas, Persia sat outside of the Roman Empire's borders, to the east. The journey from Persia to Bethlehem would cover over 1,000 miles through widely varying terrain. Scholars estimate a travel time ranging from several months to a year. Adding to that the time required for preparation, it is likely the Magi arrived in the land of King Herod some time after the first birthday of Mary's son.

## MORE THAN THREE MAGI

The typical representation of Three Wise Men arriving on camels is far from what the scene likely was. There were possibly a dozen or more Magi, riding Persian steeds, each with a retinue of soldiers and slaves. Their caravan would have been a statement of Oriental pomp and power. For these citizens of the Parthian Empire to ride into Jerusalem with their own cavalry and caravans would have been seen by Rome as an incitement to war. This is why Matthew's Gospel quickly follows up their journey to Jerusalem by saying, "When Herod the king heard this, he was troubled, and all Jerusalem with him."

Their arrival would have caused a great stir in Jerusalem. The large foreign caravan makes the ascent to the city. King Herod is informed and the strange

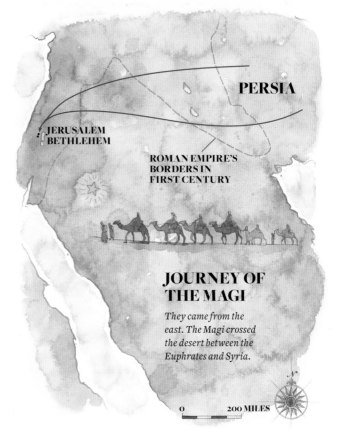

PERSIA

JERUSALEM
BETHLEHEM

ROMAN EMPIRE'S
BORDERS IN
FIRST CENTURY

## JOURNEY OF THE MAGI

*They came from the east. The Magi crossed the desert between the Euphrates and Syria.*

0        200 MILES

visitors are received into his court. We can only imagine the chill that ran down the paranoid king's spine when he heard the Magi say, "Where is He who has been born King of the Jews? For we have seen His star in the East and have come to worship Him."

Their statement was intentionally calculated to insult Herod. He saw himself as king of the Jews, and no interloper would usurp him. Herod called for a private audience with the Jews of his court to find out where such a king was to be born. Based on the prophecy of Micah, they told him Bethlehem. ◆

# { THE MAGI AND THE MESSIAH }

How did the Persian Magi learn of the ancient prophecy that a star would point the way to a king? Over the centuries, several Jews held positions of influence in the Persian court. Any or all of them could have commanded the Hebrew Scriptures be brought to them.

In the sixth century before Jesus, the Jewish prophet Daniel was made chief of the Magi in Babylon. About a century later, Nehemiah, cupbearer to King Artaxerxes I, would be in the courts of Persia. So would Esther, chosen to be queen by King Xerxes, and her cousin Mordecai.

# HEROD'S DECEPTION

IT IS THE ROMAN CENSUS THAT DRIVES MARY AND JOSEPH TO BETHLEHEM,
AND NOW A ROMAN KING FEELS THREATENED—TO THE POINT OF MADNESS.

HEROD ENGAGES THE MAGI IN CONVERSATION. HIS placid exterior veils a storm of emotion within. Herod knows nothing of this supposed king and nothing of a mysterious star pointing to his birth. He is furious but must find out more.

Even worse for Herod, the Magi declare they have seen the new king's star and have come not only to honor him but to worship him, making him a divine king and a double threat to Herod.

### KING HEROD'S PARANOIA

This period of Roman history was already awash with talk of a coming deliverer. Roman historians Tacitus and Suetonius describe a general unrest

Jewish advisers and the Magi gather around Herod in the 16th century petit-point panel. Pictured: *Visit of the Magi to Herod* Artist and date unknown

throughout the empire and the expectation of a coming deliverer who would usher in a golden age. The poets Virgil and Horace say much the same. It was an age of dissatisfaction. The boot of Rome had no shortage of agitators to crush. Even the most secure monarch was only one coup away from a toppled throne and certain death. And now these Persian Magi have taken the extreme step of a costly, arduous and time-consuming journey to see the newborn king residing in Herod's own realm.

### FINDING JESUS IN BETHLEHEM

Scholars have puzzled as to why Jesus was still in Bethlehem at this time. He most certainly spent the bulk of his childhood in Mary and Joseph's hometown of Nazareth. Yet a year or so has elapsed and they remain in Bethlehem.

Under one scenario, the family journeyed home to Nazareth shortly after Mary gave birth. Mary and Joseph make their home, and Joseph raises Jesus as his own son. This would comport with Luke's statement that they returned to Nazareth of Galilee after Jesus was presented at the temple in Jerusalem for a ritual event. Then, some time later, the family returns to Bethlehem to celebrate Passover, during which time the Wise Men arrive.

However, if the Passover was being celebrated at this time, Jerusalem would have been overrun with pilgrims, making the roads virtually impassable. The Jewish leader Philo describes the scene, saying, "Multitudes of people from a multitude of cities flow in an endless stream to the Holy Temple for each [Passover] festival…from the east and west, from the north and south." None of this is mentioned in the biblical record in association with the Wise Men's visit.

Under another scenario, Mary and Joseph simply remained in Bethlehem after the birth of Jesus. As Caesar's census wound down, the crowding would ease. Hospitality would be extended to the young family indefinitely. Infant mortality was high, and a long journey might have been inadvisable. Luke's statement of their return to Nazareth would simply be a compression of time, not uncommon in Hebrew storytelling. Under this view, the family simply remains in Bethlehem. In either case, it is in Bethlehem the Magi encounter the one they have journeyed so far to see.

### HEROD DEMANDS ANSWERS

Herod consults with his advisers and returns to the Magi. He queries them about what time the star appeared. The Magi answer truthfully, giving Herod the information he needs. Herod asks them to find the child and report back to him the location, so he can come and "worship him also." ◆

## { HEROD'S SCRIBES }

When King Herod wanted to find out where Scripture foretold that the Messiah would be born, he summoned the chief priests and the scribes. These were the religious aristocracy and the theological scholars of his day. The priests at the temple in Jerusalem not only officiated over the religious life of the Jews, they were also rulers and judges. The scribes were the experts in Scripture and the law. When asked where, according to the Scriptures, the Messiah should be born, Herod's advisers turned to the book of Micah—a prophecy written seven hundred years previously—which pointed directly to Bethlehem. It is remarkable that Herod's own advisers correctly identify Bethlehem as the city of the new king's birth, yet none of them joins the Magi's journey to find him.

*The Adoration of the Magi*
By Abraham Bloemaert
ca. 1623–24

# THE WISE MEN COME TO THE STABLE

THE MAGI'S CARAVAN DESCENDS FROM JERUSALEM,
SNAKING ALONG THE 6-MILE ROUTE TO BETHLEHEM.

THE SLEEPY LITTLE TOWN OF BETHLEHEM WOULD be utterly unaccustomed to such a visit. Dignitaries from afar enter the village. Their display of wealth and importance would turn heads. Matthew's Gospel says the star "went before them, till it came and stood over" the location of Jesus. Some credit this to a miracle. Modern astronomers might interpret this as retrograde motion of celestial bodies.

In either case, the Magi find the one they are looking for. Their excitement and joy overflow. They

are on the brink of meeting this king, signified by a heavenly star, the very object of their arduous quest. It is notable that the scriptural accounts record no hesitation by the Magi over the humble dwelling of the king.

The Gospel of Matthew describes their encounter in straightforward terms. "And when they had come into the house, they saw the young Child with Mary His mother, and fell down and worshipped Him." They are in a typical house of the region. Jesus is now called a "young child," no longer an infant. He is with his mother. They have no wealth to speak of. Jesus might be wrapped in a blanket; Mary in her typical garb. These Magi enter and, dressed in royal finery, with turbans and gowns and jewelry and crowns, touch their faces to the dirt floor, proclaiming their praises to the child. The contrast could not have been greater. Camels and steeds, porters and servants, wait outside, while inside their masters worship the most unlikely king the world has ever seen.

Though the Scriptures never say there were Three Wise Men, Matthew says they opened their treasures and presented him with three extravagant gifts—gold and two highly valued spices, frankincense and myrrh. While the Bible does not tell us the significance of these gifts, tradition has it that there is a deeper meaning for each of the three.

### GIFTS OF THE THREE KINGS
By giving gold, the Magi recognized Jesus' kingship. Gold was the most precious of metals. It represented wealth and prestige. The Magi were willing to pour their treasures at the feet of young Jesus because they saw in him the world's most glorious king.

Frankincense is a perfume or incense made from highly aromatic tree sap. When warmed, frankincense emits a fragrant aroma. It was offered on a specialized incense altar in the temple in Jerusalem. In the gift of frankincense, people of faith see Jesus as a member of a priestly order, capable of bridging the gap between God above and humans below.

Myrrh is an anointing oil from the sap of a resinous tree. This oil was used in the embalming process to perfume a body for burial. Myrrh was also provided to victims of crucifixion—a Persian invention—as a narcotic to dull the senses. Jesus would again be offered myrrh at his own death. The gift of myrrh may have been a foreshadowing of what lay ahead for this child-king and priest.

### THE MAGI DEPART
We are left with many unanswered questions. Did young Jesus fuss when the Magi arrived? What did Mary feel? Where was Joseph? What about other members of the household? No doubt, like Jerusalem, all of Bethlehem was abuzz. What is certain is that from humble Jewish shepherds to mighty gentile Magi, the Gospels depict the whole of humankind bowing before their gracious king Jesus.

The Wise Men depart for home. God warns them in a dream not to return to Herod, so they trace the long journey back to Persia by another way. ◆

## { LEGENDS OF THE MAGI }

Legend has it that the Magi became followers of Jesus and were baptized by St. Thomas. They are named Gaspar, Melchior and Balthasar in documents seven centuries after Christ. In time, other names were given them to reflect the various ethnicities telling the story of the Magi's visit.

The Eastern Orthodox Church maintains that the Holy Monastery of Saint Paul on Mount Athos, in northeastern Greece, houses part of the gifts brought to baby Jesus by the Magi. The Cologne Cathedral, located along Germany's border with the Netherlands and Belgium, has the Shrine of the Three Kings, and is said to house a relic, or fragment of the bones, of the Magi.

The Magi are often depicted on altars in churches throughout the world.

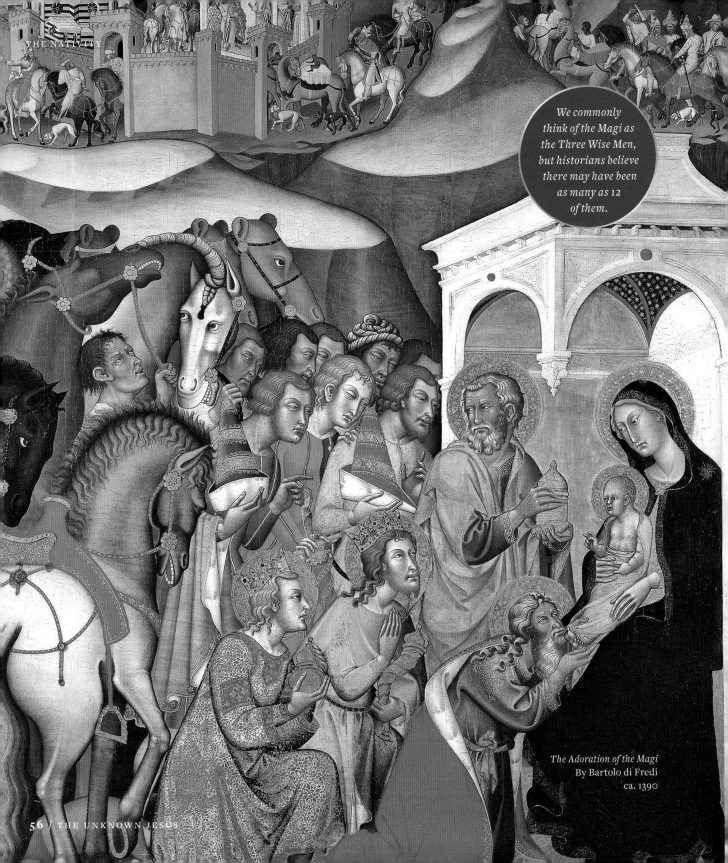

We commonly think of the Magi as the Three Wise Men, but historians believe there may have been as many as 12 of them.

The Adoration of the Magi
By Bartolo di Fredi
ca. 1390

# THE MYSTERY OF THE VANISHING MAGI

## WHERE DID THE WISE MEN GO AFTER THEY VISITED JESUS IN BETHLEHEM?

AMONG THE MANY MYSTERIES OF THE LIFE OF JESUS is the curious affair of the appearance—then the immediate disappearance—of the Three Wise Men, also known as the Magi.

First mystery: Though central figures in the Christmas story today, did you ever wonder why Matthew's Gospel is the only one of the four that mentions the Wise Men's visit to the baby Jesus? Did Mark, Luke and John not know of this visit, or simply consider it unworthy of mention?

Second mystery: One would think that the inspiration that compelled the Magi to travel great distances to worship the baby Jesus would also drive them to maintain contact with him throughout his life. And yet, after a brief description of their visit and return home, the Magi completely disappear, never to be heard from again.

It is also odd that Matthew should introduce such a moving and colorful subplot, but never follow it up. To him, was the ultimate value of the Wise Men their ability to deliver gifts to an infant?

It defies logic that these remarkable men from the East, intuitive "wise men" who "knew the prophecies," would travel long and far, following a star believing it would lead them to the newborn king of the Jews, only to drop off some gold, myrrh and frankincense—then turn around and leave forever, playing no further part in the life of the child they had come to adore.

It simply makes no sense. Wouldn't they have wished to help Mary and Joseph raise their son?

Invite him to visit their homelands? For that matter, wouldn't Mary and Joseph have wished to have stayed in touch with these extraordinary visitors?

Note that nowhere does Matthew specify that there were three kings. We infer this because there were three gifts. (And, of course, the number three has deep symbolic meaning in a religion based upon the Holy Trinity.) Some Eastern Christian traditions say there were 12 of them!

There is also no assertion that the Magi believed Jesus to be the Messiah. And it is never specified that they visited Jesus and his family immediately after the birth. The visit might have been weeks or months later, and (according to Matthew) in a home rather than a smelly stable, presumably—per custom in those days—in the guest room of a relative.

What we are told in the Bible is that the Three Wise Men were supposed to head back to Judea to tell Herod, who with treacherous motives had said he also wanted to adore the child, where Jesus was, when an angel appeared to them in a dream and warned them not to, so they "went home by a different route." That was truly wise.

Finally, it is not definitive that the Magi were actually kings. Church tradition usually considers them noblemen: Balthasar was (variously) Babylonian, Arabian or Ethiopian; Gaspar, Indian; and Melchior, Persian. The king identification may have been a way to link them to Isaiah 60:3: "Nations will come to your light, and kings to the brightness of your dawn." ◆

"Then Herod, when he saw that he was deceived by the Wise Men, was exceedingly angry…"
—Matthew 2:16

*Flight Into Egypt*
By Bartolomé Esteban Murillo
ca. 1647–50

# ESCAPE TO EGYPT

LITTLE IS CERTAIN OF THE HOLY FAMILY'S SOJOURN IN EGYPT. WHAT IS KNOWN, HOWEVER, IS THAT EVERYTHING PROCEEDED ACCORDING TO GOD'S PLAN.

ALONGSIDE ABLE ADMINISTRATION AND MAGNIFICENT building projects, the legacy of King Herod the Great is one of volatility, vanity and bloodshed. His rise to the throne was marked with violence. He murdered his wife, mother-in-law and three oldest sons to consolidate power. To Herod, life was cheap—and he would kill without hesitation to gain or maintain power.

When the Magi declared their quest to journey to see the one "born king of the Jews," Herod reacted, at first, with contained deceit. He falsely declared his intention to come and worship the child and asked for the Magi to report to him his exact location.

We are not told precisely how long Herod stayed and waited for the Magi to return to his court. After a matter of only a day or two, his anger might have boiled over. With Bethlehem located a mere 6 miles away from his palace in Jerusalem, it would not be hard for Herod to send a courier out to search for the Magi. Perhaps he sent a rider on a horse, urging him to make haste to find the Magi and to determine what was taking them so long. The 12-mile round trip would be completed in just a few hours. Herod must have been pacing his throne room, spewing his rage, waiting for the report. Frightened attendants did their best to stay out of sight.

## { HEROD'S TERROR }

Herod the Great's reign ended in terror. Not long after his visit from the Wise Men and the Massacre of the Innocents, he became ill. When rumor circulated that Herod was dying, two popular Jewish teachers, Judas and Matthias, incited their pupils to remove the huge golden eagle that Herod had placed over the most important gate of the temple in Jerusalem. The eagle offended the Jews because they saw it as a graven image, something that was prohibited by God's law. Herod's soldiers arrested about 40 of the young Jewish students involved in the removal. The dying king was so enraged at this insubordination that he ordered the rebels to be burned alive.

59

### HEROD'S PLAN IS FOILED

To the king's dismay, he would soon find out that the Wise Men had already departed, circumventing Jerusalem entirely.

What Herod cannot see is the hand of God reaching down to protect the son of Mary. An angel has descended from heaven to deliver an urgent warning to Joseph in a dream. "Flee to Egypt," the angel says. "Herod will seek the young Child to destroy him."

Joseph's response is immediate. Scripture reports they left Jerusalem that very night, traveling in darkness to escape Herod's rage. One can only imagine how they gathered their few things, said a hasty goodbye, and set out through the village as swiftly and silently as they could.

Their departure was just in time.

We can imagine Herod's spy as he covers the distance quickly. He gallops through the small town, searching for evidence of the Persian visitors. He asks the locals. They tell him the caravan has come and gone. With that, he turns his horse and races back to the palace.

The spy rushes into Herod's presence. He bows and announces his finding before his ruler: "The Magi are gone, disappeared without a trace." The king's paranoia reaches a peak. His murderous rage bursts forth in a command for the immediate slaughter of all male children in Bethlehem who are under 2 years of age.

### MASSACRE OF THE INNOCENTS

Historians have named this moment the Massacre of the Innocents. Herod's soldiers descend on Bethlehem without warning. They move from house to house, rounding up infant males and boys so young they can scarcely walk. Resistance is futile. The king's killing machine operates with remorseless efficiency.

Man's inhumanity to other human beings is fully on display. The Christmas narrative tells the unvarnished story of the evil lurking in the human heart and of the madness of unrestrained power. It is this very story Jesus was born to change, not by force but by transforming hearts through sacrificial love.

Herod would have none of this. Matthew notes he felt "mocked" by the Magi, embarrassed and humiliated by their actions. His pompous power formed a thin veneer over a weak and impetuous soul.

### WEEPING IN RAMAH

Some have suggested by setting his murderous decree at 2 years of age, Herod indicated the age of Jesus. It is more likely, however, that Jesus was closer to 1 year of age and Herod's decree was meant to ensure no possibility of error.

## { GOD SPOKE THROUGH DREAMS }

The Christmas story includes five instances of God communicating through dreams. First, an angel tells Joseph not to divorce Mary, as her child is the virgin-born, God-sent Savior. The other four dreams cluster around the visit of the Magi. God warns them not to return to Herod after visiting Jesus. An angel tells Joseph in a dream to escape to Egypt before Herod slaughters all the male babies. Later, an angel advises Joseph it is safe to return to Israel because Herod is dead. And finally, God tells Joseph to steer clear of Judea because Herod's son Archelaus is on the throne there.

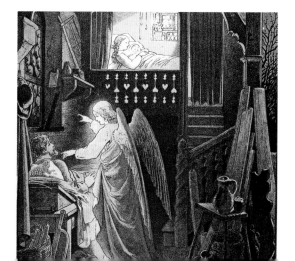

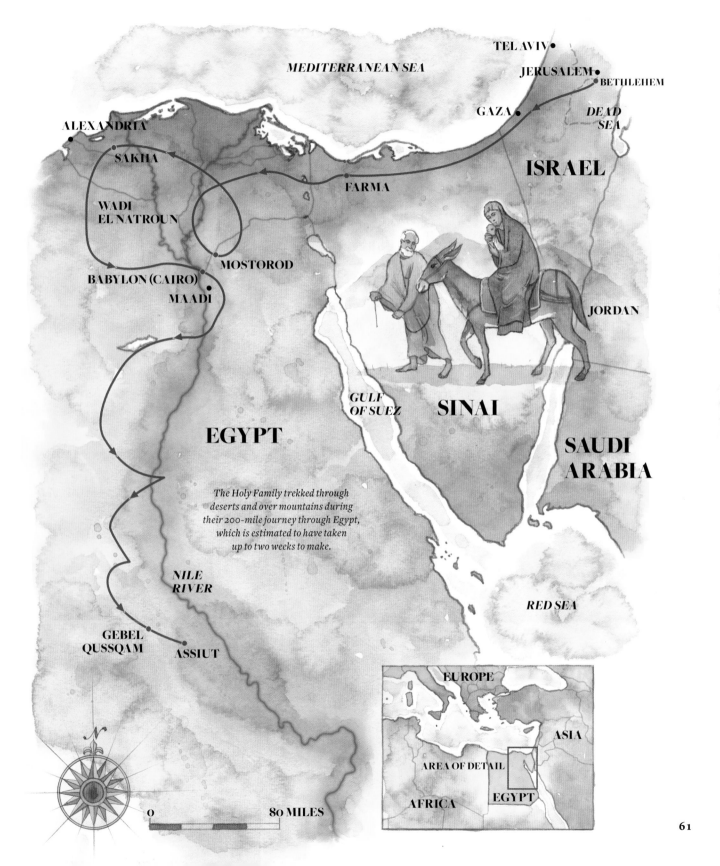

MEDITERRANEAN SEA

TEL AVIV

JERUSALEM

BETHLEHEM

GAZA

DEAD SEA

ALEXANDRIA

SAKHA

ISRAEL

WADI EL NATROUN

FARMA

MOSTOROD

BABYLON (CAIRO)

MAADI

JORDAN

GULF OF SUEZ

SINAI

SAUDI ARABIA

EGYPT

*The Holy Family trekked through deserts and over mountains during their 200-mile journey through Egypt, which is estimated to have taken up to two weeks to make.*

NILE RIVER

RED SEA

GEBEL QUSSQAM

ASSIUT

N

0        80 MILES

EUROPE

ASIA

AREA OF DETAIL

EGYPT

AFRICA

*Flight Into Egypt Altarpiece*
One of 12 panels depicting
the life of Jesus
By 15th-century artist
Jaume Ferrer II

Herod reclines on his throne even as weeping echoes over Bethlehem's hills. The Gospel of Matthew parallels this tragedy with the prophet Jeremiah's lamentation seven centuries earlier. "A voice was heard in Ramah, lamentation, weeping, and great mourning, Rachel weeping for her children, refusing to be comforted, because they are no more."

Scholars have wondered why contemporary historians like Josephus fail to report the slaughter. The likely answer, as cold as it is, could simply be that Bethlehem was too small, too out of the way, and too insignificant to merit mention. The number of boys massacred would have been relatively small—not enough to make the history books.

### OUT OF HEROD'S REACH

Now there is yet another angelic visit, another dream, and another interruption to the Holy Family's simple lives. Perhaps Mary remembers a warning she was given that a sword would pierce her soul. With Jesus safely bundled, they escape Bethlehem under the cover of night. They move quickly, probably on foot, though ancient art and iconography sometimes depict Mary riding a donkey and Jesus riding on Joseph's shoulders. Nothing can be said with certainty.

### FROM BETHLEHEM TO EGYPT

Two main routes connected Judea with Egypt. The first, called the Way of the Sea or the Great Trunk Road, lay west of Bethlehem and ran north and south along the Mediterranean Sea. Getting to this road from Bethlehem would pose problems. The shortest option would take them north, requiring them to skirt Jerusalem, then west to the Great Trunk Road, then south to Egypt. The road was well-traveled, and soldiers could appear at any moment.

The more probable route would have been straight south to Hebron and then west to the Great Trunk Road and south to Egypt. This would be the fastest, most direct route away from Jerusalem and out of Herod's reach.

The journey's length would have been up to 200 miles, depending on where they lodged in Egypt. Much of their travel would be through barren, hilly and difficult terrain. Travelers were often known to move in groups, as protection from bandits. One can only imagine how Mary and Joseph explained their flight to Egypt to fellow travelers. The trip might have taken anywhere from a few days up to two weeks.

The Christmas story is painted in sharply contrasting hues. The beauty of a mother and child is set against the disruption of a mandatory census. The wonder of angelic hosts in heaven stands out against the slaughter of innocent boys.

**STORIES OF JESUS IN EGYPT ABOUND**
Since most of the towns in Egypt had sizable Jewish populations, Mary, Joseph and Jesus would have been warmly received.

The only definitive source reporting this journey is Matthew's Gospel, which offers virtually no detail. However, other stories quickly arose. The historicity of these stories cannot be verified.

In one, the fourth-century Coptic pope, Theophilus, 23rd patriarch of Alexandria, announced he had been visited by the Virgin Mary in a vision, where she recounted details of her journey. These are recorded in the apocryphal Vision of Theophilus.

An early third-century theologian, Hippolytus of Rome, reported the Holy Family remained in Egypt for three-and-a-half years. In one account, when Mary, Joseph and Jesus reach Egypt, they are attacked by robbers. Jesus has a silver sandal stolen. Mary is upset. To care for her, young Jesus draws the sign of a cross on the ground and a spring immediately bubbles up. The waters were said to have healing powers.

Other stories speak of palm trees bowing as the Holy Family passed by. In another account, idols fell down and shattered when Jesus was present. Yet another tells of a sacred tree growing from a single drop of Jesus' sweat. Lions and leopards adored him, and roses blossomed wherever he appeared.

These legends bear little resemblance to the simplicity and gritty realism of the Gospel accounts and are of questionable historical validity.

{ **NO TRACES REMAIN** }

No historical traces remain of the Holy Family's visit to Egypt. The Coptic Orthodox Church of Alexandria, the ancient church of Egypt, suggests about two dozen locations where Jesus stayed during his time in that land. These include places where it is said Jesus caused a water spring to well up or a shade tree to grow, and are based on visions, oral traditions, and writings from much later periods. The Church of the Virgin Mary, in the Al Muharraq Monastery, is built around a cave where legend says the angel appeared to Joseph in a dream and told him he was safe to return to Israel. Saints Sergius and Bacchus Church, a fourth-century church in Old Cairo, sits above a cave where it is claimed that Mary, Joseph and young Jesus took shelter.

The simple carpenter and the humble mother from Nazareth now find themselves making a life in faraway Egypt as political refugees, all because a baby named Jesus was born.

### RETURNING HOME

Josephus reports yet another episode of psychotic evil from the dying despot. Fearing that no one would mourn at his death, Herod ordered the leaders of Judea to be gathered into a theater in Jericho. Once assembled, he ordered they be kept imprisoned until his death. Then, they were to be slaughtered. He wanted to ensure there would be no rejoicing at his inevitable demise. Instead, there would be mourning, even if it were not for him.

Upon Herod's death, his sister, Salome, rescinded his order and released the Jewish leaders. When Herod died in Jericho, the Romans mourned and the Jews rejoiced.

### HEROD'S SUCCESSORS

Herod the Great treated his family better in death than he had in life. In his last will and testament—later modified by Rome—the kingdom of Judea was divided among three of his sons. He left Archelaus with half the kingdom and the title of "king." Archelaus would govern Judea and Samaria and regions to the south and east. Antipas was appointed tetrarch of Galilee, the land Jesus would eventually call home. Philip inherited rule over outlying regions to the north.

### THE HOLY FAMILY MOVES TO NAZARETH

After Herod died, an angel appeared to Joseph in a dream. Those who sought to kill Jesus were dead, the angel said. The time had come for Mary and Joseph, with the little boy Jesus, to now make another journey and settle into yet another home. This time, they would at long last be home in Israel.

The biblical record indicates Joseph intended to return to Judea, most likely to Bethlehem, to take up residence. But he heard that Herod Archelaus had inherited the throne of Judea, and coupled with another divine dream, he changed plans. Archelaus was known for the same cruel disposition as his father. Within 10 years, his rule would be so brutal that the Jews would conspire to drive Archelaus out and Rome would banish him to Gaul. But with him on the throne of Judea for now, it would be unwise to bring Jesus under his jurisdiction.

## { HEROD ANTIPAS }

The story of Herod Antipas, son of Herod the Great, will be forever entwined with that of Jesus. He ruled from 4 B.C. till A.D. 39. The Bible presents him as suspicious, foxlike in his cunning, and completely immoral. When John the Baptist, son of Elizabeth and Zacharias, condemned Antipas' adulterous relationship, he had John's head cut off. Later, Antipas would make mockery over Jesus, cynically suggesting his movement was John the Baptist all over again. The Pharisees, perhaps wanting Jesus out of town, advised him to leave because Antipas wanted him killed. At his trial, Jesus refused to speak a word to Antipas, who mocked him and sent him back to Pontius Pilate, governor of Judea, who ordered Jesus' crucifixion.

*The Return From Egypt*
By Giovanni Francesco Romanelli
ca. 1635

Mary and Joseph head instead toward Galilee, the northern province, and to Nazareth, the city of their upbringing, under the rule of Herod Antipas, a largely uninvolved despot.

With King Herod's threat no longer hanging over Jesus, they would have taken the most direct route to Nazareth. The Way of the Sea, the Via Maris, led directly from Egypt to Galilee, skirting close to Nazareth. This journey would be their longest yet. But by this time, Jesus was walking and talking, and the burden of travel would have been eased.

The road would take them northward, through Gaza, Ashkelon, Joppa and Megiddo. They were walking the path the patriarchs walked 2,000 years earlier. They would cover over 300 miles as the crow flies, and up to 500 miles on the winding roads, in a journey lasting a couple of weeks.

At long last, they reach Nazareth, the place they would call home for the rest of Jesus' childhood and into his adulthood. Matthew's Gospel would tie the return to the ancient prophetic voice of God in Hosea, saying, "Out of Egypt, I have called my son."

Neither Mary nor Joseph would have ever planned their lives as they unfolded. But God's wisdom is evident in every move, and they knew well enough to entrust their lives into his omnipotent and gracious hands. ◆

When Jesus, then 12, explained
God's thinking in the Scriptures
to assorted rabbis, they were
amazed at hìs incisiveness.
Pictured: *Christ Among the Doctors*
By Orazio Borgianni
ca. 1609

# 3

## The Lost Years

# WHAT WE KNOW ABOUT CHRIST'S BOYHOOD

WE INVARIABLY FOCUS ON JESUS' BIRTH, HIS SHORT MINISTRY AND THE EVENTS SURROUNDING HIS DEATH. BUT WHAT HAPPENED IN THE MANY YEARS THAT CAME BETWEEN THESE EVENTS? SCHOLARS REMAIN LARGELY MYSTIFIED.

THE STORIES ABOUT JESUS BEGIN, WELL, AT THE beginning.

The birthplace of Jesus was probably not the Bethlehem of Judea, despite the accounts of Matthew and Luke's Gospels—and many Christmas carols.

In Matthew 2:1–2, it reads: "When Jesus was born in Bethlehem of Judea, in the days of King Herod, behold, Magi from the East arrived in Jerusalem, saying, 'Where is the newborn king of the Jews? We saw his star at its rising and have come to do him homage.'"

Luke 2:4–7 reads: "And Joseph also went up from Galilee, from the town of Nazareth, to Judea, to the city of David, which is called Bethlehem, because he was of the house and lineage of David, to be registered with Mary, his betrothed, who was with child. And while they were there, the time came for

This image captures Mary and Joseph's emotions at finding their 12-year-old son after losing him for three days.

*The Finding of the Saviour in the Temple*
By William Holman Hunt
ca. 1854-60

69

*Coming Home From the
Flight to Egypt With the
Saints Catherine and Francis*
By Benedetto Marini
ca. 1620

her to give birth. And she gave birth to her firstborn son and wrapped him in swaddling clothes and laid him in a manger, because there was no place for them in the inn."

But few scholars unaffiliated with Christian churches think that there is any truth to these stories. Tony Burke, PhD, a professor in the Department of Humanities at York University in Ontario, Canada, says these birth stories are not historical: "Matthew and Luke place Jesus' birth in Bethlehem only to connect Jesus with traditions about David, so they construct infancy narratives that place him there, if only temporarily."

The significance of Bethlehem (which is located only 5 miles from Jerusalem) was that it was the birthplace of King David. It had been prophesied that the Messiah would be a direct descendant of David, which is why Matthew and Luke took such pains to identify Jesus' birthplace as Bethlehem in their Gospels.

Burke goes on to explain that the Church of the Nativity in Bethlehem of Judea was built over a cave in the fourth century, a time when Christianity was establishing pilgrimage sites for every story in the Bible, and even stories not found in the Bible.

"No stone was untouched by Jesus, no cave was wasted as a possible location of interest," says Burke. "That Jesus was born in a cave is a tradition tied to Justin Martyr [a philosopher said to be the foremost expert on the Divine Word, whose name tells his end story—he followed Christianity with such fervor he was executed] around A.D. 150, and shows up also in the Protevangelium [Gospel] of James, a very popular noncanonical text about the births of Jesus and his mother, Mary."

Since Justin seems to be aware of the location of this cave, says Burke, it is possible that the location's connection to Jesus' birth was a very early tradition, but that is no guarantee that it truly is Jesus' birthplace.

So where *was* Jesus actually born? According to Burke, "The Gospels of Mark and John both tell us that Jesus is from Nazareth." (Mark 1:9 and 6:1, John 1:45–56 and 7:41–42) More precisely, they mean Bethlehem of the Galilee, just 4 miles from Nazareth. This makes more sense, according to many scholars, historians and archaeologists because they find it hard to believe Joseph and Mary, who was then nine months pregnant, would have traveled 68 miles from Nazareth to Bethlehem of Judea, Joseph's hometown.

FOR THE REST OF JESUS' UPBRINGING, ALL SCHOLARS can do to fill in the blanks about their family life in Nazareth is to turn to other sources.

"I think children in a Galilean village would have had shortened childhoods, or at least would have been introduced to work as soon as they were able," says James Strange, PhD, professor of New Testament at Samford University in Birmingham, Alabama. Strange believes that Jesus worked alongside Joseph at various tasks and could load and drive a donkey, and unload it at the destination.

## "GALILEE UNDER ROMAN OCCUPATION HAD A FAIRLY ROBUST ECONOMY."
—James Strange, PhD

"Contrary to older views, in which people thought of the Galileans as peasants who barely escaped starvation year by year, who were landlocked, rarely traveling outside of their own villages and who would never set foot in a city, we now know that Galilee, under Roman occupation, had a fairly robust economy in which people did indeed travel both to the city and from village to village, whether to engage in commerce or to find work," Strange, who leads archaeological excavations in Israel, said in a 2016 interview in *Ancient Jew Review*.

"Mark's Gospel calls Jesus a carpenter or craftsman," says Burke, "and Matthew and Luke, who introduce us to Joseph, say that he was a carpenter also. And given the interest in peasant life found in Jesus' parables, it is likely he came from humble origins. He would have been trained in his father's trade and perhaps attended school beginning at the age of 5. Students showing promise would go onto further studies and, given Jesus' command of Scripture, he may have done so, though he may have been obligated instead to work."

"I think he was neither poor nor well off," says Strange, who believes it's unlikely that anyone then had a single job. "The tradition that Joseph was a carpenter, and hence that Jesus was too, is built on a single verse in Matthew: 'Is not this the carpenter's son?' [13:55]. To call Joseph a 'carpenter' means that, when he wasn't engaged in farming or animal husbandry or other tasks, his specialty was carpentry."

## "HE STOOD UP TO READ, AND THE SCROLL OF THE PROPHET ISAIAH WAS HANDED TO HIM."
—Luke 4:16–17

Another skill Jesus and other children of Galilee had was the ability to read. "Luke depicts Jesus reading from the scroll of Isaiah in the Nazareth synagogue [4:16–20]," says Strange. "Jesus would have been taught to read Hebrew Scriptures—probably learning to read in the synagogue where the scrolls were housed."

Strange adds that it is likely that most villages of Jesus' day had synagogues, and the reading of Torah was an important practice there. Strange points to the Magdala Stone, a carved block with symbols, including a menorah, that dates back to the Second Temple (between 516 B.C. to A.D. 70) that was unearthed in the synagogue at Magdala in 2009. It's said to be a connection between the Christian and Jewish faiths, and it probably served as the base for a reading podium. Scholars believe Magdala is Mary Magdalene's hometown and that Jesus taught in the synagogue.

"We don't know if girls were also taught, or only (or mainly) boys," adds Strange. "This is one way I think that village life in Jewish Judea and Galilee would have differed from village life elsewhere in the Empire."

Otherwise, "life in a Galilean village was not so different as life elsewhere in the Roman Empire, and considering the time and the contingencies (morbidity and mortality rates), life was not considered to be too difficult, although you and I would probably not like it very much," says Strange.

Jesus' father was Joseph, but, says Strange, we don't truly know much about who he is or what he did. His lineage is detailed in both Matthew 1:1–16 and Luke 3:23–38, but the two Gospels don't see eye to eye on the subject. However, Strange points out there are lots of similarities: "Matthew begins with Abraham and moves forward to Jesus, in the way biblical lineages do, whereas Luke begins with Jesus and moves backward to Adam and thence to God." Both Gospels include King David and Abraham in Joseph's lineage.

Strange points out that Joseph was not around when Jesus was an adult, which may indicate that he died before Jesus began his ministry. "He is the main actor in the infancy narrative in Matthew (the angel communicates to him and he obeys three times) while Mary is silent, whereas Joseph is silent in Luke's infancy narrative while Mary speaks with the Angel Gabriel. Matthew depicts him as a righteous man. When people from Nazareth refer to him during Jesus' ministry, it is always as Jesus' father, or rather that Jesus is his son."

Burke says these stories aren't historically accurate, explaining that once the Gospels eventually chosen to be included in the New Testament became popular—around the middle of the second century—Christians with a gift of storytelling began to expand upon them, filling in some more of the details about the lives of Jesus and those around him. Some of these tales of Jesus' childhood are found in a text now called the Infancy Gospel of Thomas (see page 75).

According to the Rev. Johann Roten, S.M., of the University of Dayton in Ohio, an internationally recognized scholar and authority on Mary, the scenes in the Infancy Gospel have a single purpose: "He is to

A painting of the Holy
Family in the Chiesa di
San Benedetto, Italy
Artist and date unknown

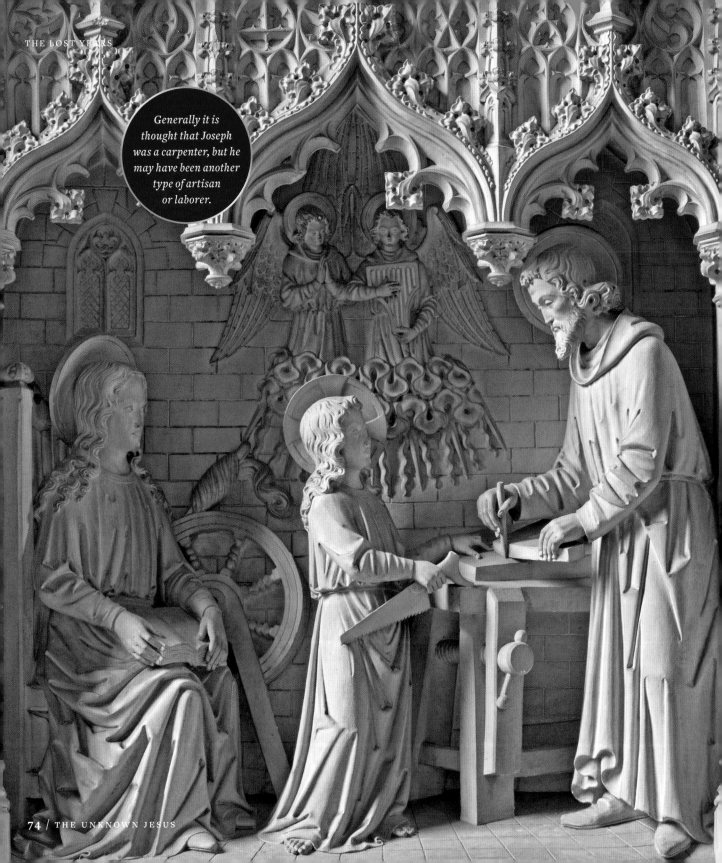

*Generally it is thought that Joseph was a carpenter, but he may have been another type of artisan or laborer.*

be shown to the world as one who has superhuman power. He gives life to the clay sparrows, is master of the Sabbath, and shows at an early age that His knowledge is that of the God-Man. Jesus is a healer and restores health and even life."

Burke describes the stories as having the feel of folktales, but agrees that the goal is showing that their subject is superhuman in some sense: "So the childhood stories of Jesus do not tell us anything about what Jesus actually did as a child, but they do reflect some aspects of life for children in the ancient world, such as a parent's desire to have his son be educated or learn a trade, or to behave appropriately and bring the family honor, not shame."

Some of the plots are highly unlikely: The boy who became the man who understood himself to be the Son of God is not likely to have hurt anyone. ◆

## { THE INFANCY GOSPEL } Thomas tells stories of Jesus' childhood.

### JESUS MAKES SPARROWS

When Jesus was 5 years old, he was playing near a stream with other children. He created pools of dirty water and ordered them to become clean and clear. He then took soft clay from the mud and formed 12 sparrows. This took place on the Sabbath, which wasn't permissible. One of the children went and told Joseph about this act. When Joseph came and questioned Jesus about why he was doing this, Jesus responded by clapping his hands and telling the birds to fly away. They did, which everyone witnessed. In the Arabic Infancy Gospel, which scholars believe was written sometime in the fifth and sixth centuries and is based on other fictional documents, Jesus was 7 when he made birds out of clay. One boy who told his parents about this was told not to play with this wizard anymore!

### RAISING ZENO

Jesus was playing with children on a roof when one of them, Zeno, fell off and died. Jesus was accused by the boy's parents of pushing him. Jesus came down from the roof, called out Zeno's name, and stated, "Rise and say whether I pushed you down." Zeno rose and said no.

### JESUS THE HEALER

A man was splitting wood when he split his foot open with his ax, bled out and died. Jesus held the man's foot in his hand and it healed immediately and he returned to life.

### CURSING A BOY

There are stories about Jesus attacking or disparaging one of several other boys. He cursed them and they either died or became incapacitated. Not very Christian, you might say!

When a child complained about the pools and Jesus made them go away, Jesus proclaimed, "Your fruit (will have) no root, and your shoot will be withered like a scorched branch in a violent wind!" Then the child immediately withered away. While leaving with Joseph, Jesus felt someone strike his shoulder. He turned and cried, "Cursed be you because of your leader!" And the child died immediately. (We're not buying this one...)

### JAMES' SNAKEBITE

While Jesus and his brother James were out gathering sticks, James' hand was bitten by a viper. Jesus blew on it and it was healed. The snake was obliterated. Can't say we feel too badly about the snake.

### CURING A SICK CHILD

Jesus heard a woman crying because her baby was dying. Jesus ran over quickly, touched the infant's chest and entreated him to not die, but to live and be with his mother. The child looked up and laughed. Jesus told the mother to give her baby milk and to remember him. The bystanders claimed Jesus was a God or an angel "because his every word becomes a deed." Jesus then went back to playing with his friends.

PERCEPTION VS. REALITY

# DID JESUS HAVE SIBLINGS?

HISTORIANS THINK IT'S PROBABLE, AND THE GOSPELS LIST AT LEAST
SIX BROTHERS AND SISTERS. BUT THERE'S NOT MUCH KNOWN ABOUT
THE FAMILY MEMBERS WHO WITNESSED HIS CHILDHOOD.

THE GOSPELS SAY JESUS HAD FOUR BROTHERS (James, Joseph, Simon and Judas) and at least two sisters—a typical size for a family of the time. The sisters are unnamed in the Gospels. "The idea that they are children of Joseph from a previous marriage is part of Catholic doctrine that Mary remained a virgin," says James Strange, PhD. "In the New Testament, we really only learn anything about James, who became the leader of the church in Jerusalem after a persecution drove early Christians out of the city."

James—who some say is the son of *a* Mary, but not *the* Mary, and is perhaps a cousin of Jesus—along with his siblings, did not believe that Jesus was the Messiah (John 7:5 reads: "For even his brothers did not believe in him"). Scripture shows they were not present during his crucifixion.

"None are depicted as a disciple of Jesus during his ministry," says Strange. The full verse in John 7:5, in fact, has his siblings openly mocking Jesus: "His brothers therefore said to him, 'Depart from here and go into Judea, that your disciples also may see the works that you are doing. For no one does anything in secret while he himself seeks to be known openly. If you do these things, show yourself to the world.'"

According to Mark 6:4, Jesus responds: "A prophet is not without honor except in his own country, among his own relatives, and in his own house."

In addition to his visiting the temple at 12 years old, there are actually many stories about Jesus' childhood—but they don't appear in the four sanctioned Gospels that make up the biblical canon.

"The earliest account of Jesus' childhood is found in a text now called the Infancy Gospel of

> "*A PROPHET IS NOT WITHOUT HONOR EXCEPT IN HIS OWN COUNTRY, AMONG HIS OWN RELATIVES.*"
> —Mark 6:4

Thomas (page 75), though its original title was simply the Childhood of Jesus," says Tony Burke, PhD, a professor in the Department of Humanities at York University in Ontario, Canada, who studies the writings. "It tells stories of Jesus from the ages of 5 to 12. Some aspects of the stories are familiar activities of Jesus: He interacts with his parents and his brother, he heals the sick and injured, he displays wisdom. But some seem peculiar, even offensive to modern readers: He maims and kills anyone who crosses him, including playmates and teachers." ◆

*Holy Family* fresco in St. Michael parish church, Sebechleby, Slovakia
By Jozef Antal
1963

Unlike other females of their time, Jewish women like Mary may have been literate. Here, she reads to Jesus.

In one of the final passages of his childhood, Jesus is found teaching rabbinical scholars.

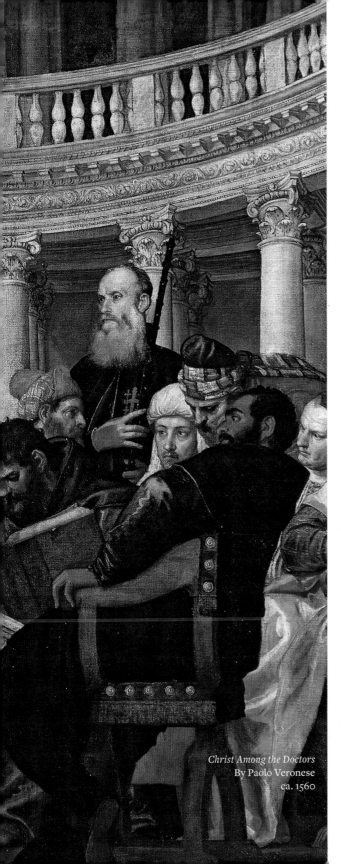

*Christ Among the Doctors*
By Paolo Veronese
ca. 1560

# HIS
## LITTLE-KNOWN YOUTH

ONE OF THE GREAT MYSTERIES IS WHAT JESUS DID BETWEEN TEACHING IN THE SYNAGOGUE AT AGE 12 AND STARTING HIS MINISTRY AT 30.

COUNTLESS COMMENTARIES DEAL WITH THE ENIGMA of Jesus the man, and his mysterious, almost total absence from recorded history during a crucial 30 years of his life. Theories range from sober historical research by respected scholars and theologians to wildly fantastic flights of imagination (Jesus as an extraterrestrial, a teacher from another dimension, and so on; it gets wacky).

The story begins innocently enough. The Gospel of Luke (2:40) tells us: "The child grew, and waxed strong in spirit, filled with wisdom; and the grace of God was upon him."

But how to interpret this? Does it suggest that, even as a child, Jesus was already the Christ? If so, to what extent would he—still a child, then an adolescent—have been aware of that?

Luke (2:49) offers a tantalizing clue: Following Jewish custom, when Jesus was 12, he traveled with his family to Jerusalem to celebrate Passover. By tradition, a boy was automatically a bar mitzvah ("Son of the Commandments") at that age, and could take his place among the men in Jewish rituals.

*Christ Among the Doctors*
By Diego de la Cruz
ca. 1495–97

At the end of that Passover, Mary and Joseph set out to return home.

The men traveled together in one group, with the women going separately. Apparently each parent thought that Jesus was traveling with the other's party. (This is not implausible: Until recently, Jesus had been considered a child, therefore he presumably would have been traveling with the women. But at this point he had become a man in the eyes of the other men.) After three days, Mary and Joseph discovered that Jesus was not traveling with either group, so they returned to look for him.

They found Jesus in the synagogue, discussing the Hebrew Scriptures—as an adult would—with rabbinical scholars. (The "Finding in the Temple" is one of the Joyful Mysteries celebrated in the Rosary.) According to Luke, Jesus asked his parents: "Why were you seeking me? Did you not know that I must be about my father's business?"

Many theologians interpret this as a sign that, even as a 12-year-old boy, Jesus was aware he had some divine purpose. This, in turn, implies that he was already conscious of being imbued with the Christ Spirit. Might it also mean that Jesus was at that moment actually beginning his ministry on Earth? Such a mission would very likely require him to leave his earthly parents' home, and travel the world, spreading his heavenly message.

The Gospels are silent regarding specific details. This leaves much open to speculation, including the idea he visited India and Tibet (see page 81).

But contemporary Christian scholars generally dismiss most of these distant travel scenarios, and assert, not that helpfully, that nothing is known for certain about the 18 missing years. The great likelihood is that Jesus spent his youth from age 12 to 29 in and around Galilee, learning and then practicing his father's trade as a carpenter, living a normal life like other young men in the community.

Luke tells us that after Jesus' visit to the temple: "And he went down [with his parents], and came to Nazareth, and was subject unto them: but his mother kept all these sayings in her heart. And Jesus increased in wisdom and stature, and in favor with God and man" (Luke 2:51, 52).

Whether this included marrying and raising a family, which would normally be expected of young Jews, has been a matter of controversy for millennia. The Church says no; agnostic historians tend to think he must have. It will remain as elusive an enigma as the Jewel in the Lotus. It is another aspect of the Magnum Mysterium—the Great Mystery—that is Jesus of Nazareth.

If Jesus had performed any miracles or given any major sermons during this time, we would expect to find a record of it somewhere. But his first recorded miracle was his reluctant one at the wedding at Cana; no other action is attributed to him between the teaching in the temple and that event. ◆

## {JESUS AND KRISHNA} Is there a connection…or just coincidence?

The notion of Indian thought influencing Jesus was first proposed in Louis Jacolliot's influential 1869 book *La Bible Dans l'Inde* ("The Bible in India"), subtitled *Vie de Iezeus Christna* ("Life of Jesus Christ"). Jacolliot stopped short of claiming that Jesus actually traveled to India, as others have done. But he does compare accounts of the life of Bhagavan Krishna, who is believed to be the eighth incarnation of the Hindu God Vishnu, with that of Jesus. Based on the remarkable similarity of many details in both stories, Jacolliot contends that the Gospels may well be myths that are based on earlier histories of ancient India.

There is a theory that Jesus went to India to study Hinduism, but it's unlikely he made such a journey.

# DID JESUS TRAVEL TO FAR-FLUNG LANDS?

## SOME SPECULATE HE WENT TO TIBET AND INDIA—AND EVEN ENGLAND. BUT IT'S VERY IMPROBABLE.

AMONG THE MANY WELL-WORN THEORIES OF JESUS' activities during the missing years is that he traveled to distant lands, seeking knowledge from Buddhists in Tibet; studying with Hindu masters in India, priests of Egypt or wise men in other remote places; or staying closer to home, to train with the Essenes (an ascetic sect) in the Judean desert. One medieval legend even suggested that Jesus visited England as a young boy to study with the Druids! Any of these trips would have been a formidable undertaking.

Consider the purely logistical aspects of travel at that time: There were few well-established, reliable roads for long-distance trips. Overland transport was limited to walking, camelback, horse-drawn carts, or a combination of these. Traveling these kind of distances would require an enormous amount of time.

On foot, people might have covered about 20 miles a day. Let's assume that a camel could average as much as 65 miles a day. The distance from Israel to Tibet, for example, is about 3,200 miles, give or take a mountain or two. If the trip were entirely on flat terrain—and the Himalayas are not even remotely flat—the trip would have lasted about 160 days one way on foot or 49 on a camel, assuming no mishaps.

The route from the River Jordan to the Indus River in India is about 2,900 miles—a demanding journey, much of it through a camel-challenging, irregular landscape. It's very unlikely such a trek was undertaken by Jesus, and extremely unlikely not to have been referenced in the main Gospels if he had.

And what is the likelihood that a teenager, even a highly motivated, exceptionally well-prepared one, would choose to overcome such daunting geographical obstacles to seek wisdom in distant lands, whose languages and customs he could not have known?

Moreover, where would Jesus, a humble carpenter living in a village in the Judean desert, have learned of a wisdom so great, possibly so superior to that of the Hebrews, that it would be worth his traveling all across the known world to study? There's no evidence of Tibetan or Indian philosophy having reached all the way to Judea.

There are other considerations as well. To accomplish such a voyage, Jesus would most likely have had to follow one of several paths of the Silk Road that crisscrossed the Near East and Asia, which allowed for international exchange of commerce, cultures (and occasionally invasions). Plus he would have needed money to fund this undertaking, another obstacle for a humble workingman.

Those who promote the "distant travels" theory might suggest that God could have whisked Jesus anywhere he wanted to go, and endowed him with the ability to instantly speak any language. But we have no sense of a helping Father intervening in Jesus' life on Earth. So we must contemplate what a young carpenter traveling in a human body, with normal human skill sets and limits, in a time and place where people did limited traveling, could have achieved. ◆

It's unlikely Jesus traveled the Silk Road, a trade route, that connected the Mediterranean with East Asia.

A Russian icon shows Jesus among the rabbis in the synagogue. Jesus was known as the greatest rabbi, and no one who heard him speak wasn't amazed—even if sometimes begrudgingly so. Artist and date unknown

CHAPTER

4

*Jesus' Hebrew Heritage*

# CHRIST WAS A JEW

HE MAY NOT BE ON THE MOUNT RUSHMORE OF HEBREWS WITH THE LIKES OF ABRAHAM, MOSES AND MEL BROOKS, BUT JESUS WAS BORN A JEW, LIVED AS ONE AND EVEN DIED AS ONE. BUT HOW JEWISH WAS HE? AND WHAT WAS THAT JEWISHNESS LIKE?

LET'S START WITH HIS NAME. THE NAME JESUS HAS been bastardized through several translations. The English word *Jesus* comes to us through Greek and then Latin. "If we assume that the lingua franca in Galilee in the early first century was Hebrew or Aramaic, then he seems to have been called Yeshua, which is a shortened form of Yehoshua," says Paul V.M. Flesher, PhD, director of religious studies at the University of Wyoming. "The latter word renders into English as Joshua."

If he had any other names associated with him, it was "ben Joseph," according to Flesher, which means "son of Joseph."

Christ is an anglicization of *Xristos*, which is Greek for "anointed one" and has generally been changed over time into "messiah." Christ is not Jesus' surname. In ancient Judaism, Flesher explains, messiahs were thought to be anointed, but many other social and religious categories of people were also anointed, including priests and kings. "It is a title, not a name," Flesher says. "Technically, we should say in English, 'Jesus the Christ' in the same way we say, 'Jesus the Messiah.'"

This image of Nazareth depicts how the city may have looked during Jesus' time.

And like any Jewish male, Jesus was circumcised, as related in Luke 2:21–24: "After eight days had passed, it was time to circumcise the child, he was called Jesus, the name given by the angel before he was conceived in the womb. Then the time came for their purification according to the Law of Moses. They brought him up to Jerusalem and presented him to the Lord (as is written in the Law of the Lord, 'every firstborn male shall be designated as holy to the Lord') and they offered a sacrifice according to what is stated in the law of the Lord, a pair of turtle doves with two young pigeons." (For more on Jesus being brought to the temple, see page 94.)

### TEACHING THE TORAH

Jesus was a rabbi, but not in the institutional sense we know today. The word *rabbi* simply means "my master" and was not limited to use in a religious sense. Says Flesher: "It could apply to any master in an apprentice system, for instance. A fisherman or a carpenter could be called rabbi—'my master.'"

Jesus clearly was educated, says James Strange, PhD, professor of biblical and religious studies at Samford University in Birmingham, Alabama, and the director of the Shikhin Excavation Project in Israel. "I don't see any reason to be suspicious of Gospel accounts of Jesus reading from the Book of Isaiah and commenting on it. And if he could do it, there are other people educated enough who could. A lot of people think it's Luke reading back from an urban Christianity that exists [in Luke's time] and imposing that on Galilee. But all of our synagogue excavations show that the reading of Torah happened regularly. Jesus is literate enough to read from the scroll."

Because Jesus was a rabbi, the Gospel writers wanted to focus on his teachings and parables and the impending kingdom of God. "A lot has been said that Jesus was an apocalyptic preacher and prophet," says Strange. "He's presented as a miracle worker in all the Gospels and one that's never disputed is his debate in Torah." He was discussing two main issues: What are explicit exceptions to Torah observances, such as when can I violate the Sabbath? And what's the greatest commandment?

In Matthew 22:36–40, Jesus is asked: "Teacher, which is the greatest commandment in the Law?" He cites Deuteronomy 6:5: "Love the Lord your God with all your heart and with all your soul and with all your mind." This is the first and greatest commandment. And the second is from Leviticus 19:18: "Love your neighbor as yourself."

## { MAKING OFFERINGS }

The sacrificial system was ordained by God and placed at the very center and heart of Jewish life. The Old Testament Book of Leviticus details sacrifices ranging from whole oxen to various grains, which would often be burned as a way to atone for sins, enjoy God's fellowship, or become "clean." For her purification, Mary offered two turtle doves, a sign of both her devotion and her family's limited means. With one turtledove, a priest presented a sin offering, a sign of forgiveness with God. With the other, a priest presented a burned offering, a sign of restored fellowship from God. The Old Testament regulations for offerings and sacrifices prefigure the significance of Jesus' sacrifice.

The Lamb of God spread the biblical teachings of loving others as much as you love yourself.

*The Good Shepherd*
By Philippe de Champaigne
ca. 1650–60

Pilate sent Jesus to Herod because he was a Galilean Jew and thus under his jurisdiction. Wall painting in the Saint Fargeau church, France.

Jesus is quoting the Torah, so people agreed with him, says Strange; it would not have been considered to be controversial.

In addition to teaching the Torah, Jesus was considered a carpenter, which back in those days generally meant an artisan—anything from a carpenter to a stonemason. "That means he has some skills," says Strange. In 4 B.C., around the time Jesus was born, the city of Sepphoris was destroyed, and when Herod the Great died, the citizens of the city revolted. Strange posits that Jesus' father Joseph was probably part of the rebuilding of the city.

Years later, when Galilee was built in A.D. 18, Jesus' skills would have been needed. "As a carpenter, you're building forms for arches; if you're a mason you're cutting stone. It's reasonable that villagers have many skills. If you're a farmer, you can't farm all the time. Maybe you're a potter too," says Strange.

**CULTURAL IDEALS**

Judaism had already been around for a few thousand years before Jesus. But Flesher explains there were three types of Judaism throughout the early first century: Jerusalem and its temple-based Judaism; Galilee and its Judaism that was oriented toward Jerusalem but without any direct, immediate contact with it; and diaspora Judaism, i.e., the religion as practiced outside Israel.

Strange says that Jews in Judea, in Galilee up north as well as the nearby Golan Heights all had a similar set of views and practices. "They cared about purity and their daily lives and the

> ## "[THE JEWS OF JUDEA, GALILEE AND THE GOLAN HEIGHTS] CARED ABOUT PURITY."
>
> —*James Strange, PhD,*
> *professor of biblical and religious studies*

mikvehs—the ritual baths—associated with their homes and industries." We never hear about Jesus going to a mikveh, "but he never criticizes it," Strange points out.

The Jews of the time were also known to "engage in a type of burial called secondary burial where they intern corpses and come back a year later and collect bones and put them in a box called an ossuary," adds Strange.

## { WHAT DID JESUS EAT? } Like other Jews of his time, he kept kosher.

James Strange, PhD, definitely thinks Jesus kept kosher: He would have eaten the standard diet of Judeans of his time: wheat products like bread, a lot of vegetables and legumes, herbs and spices, and some meat. In the Gospels, Jesus tells his disciples to prepare the Passover, so they're probably getting lamb. "If he's eating meat, it's probably part of a stew," Strange surmises. "He has access to fish, probably to poultry, though that's not mentioned in the text. He's probably also eating sheep and goats; cows are primarily working animals that produce milk, so he's also eating cheese." Like all observant Jews, "he's

avoiding pork and eating kosher animals—those that are butchered and slaughtered according to known kosher practices.

"He's also going to be eating a lot of olive oil," says Strange. "We're always finding olive presses on our excavations." And definitely wine as well, says Strange, since there was wine at the Last Supper.

Occasionally, he implicitly criticized the rabbis, pointing out that it's not just about what goes into your body. "For him, the idea of keeping kosher is not just keeping clean, but to observe Torah," Strange says.

Although Galileans didn't have day-to-day contact with Jerusalem, the city was on their radar. "If they could, they would make a pilgrimage," says Strange. "One clue is that [at Shikhin, where he directs an archaeological dig], we find 'Herodian lamps'—which are not like menorahs, they're not decorated, they just have a couple of lines or small circles on the nozzle. If you analyze the clay of the lamps, many come from Jerusalem, which means some are locally made. The hypothesis is that [Jews were] bringing them back from Jerusalem."

During Jesus' time, the Romans ruled, but Flesher points out Jesus did not discuss politics very much. "Galilee was not as heavily occupied as Judea; there

## "MAN SHALL NOT LIVE BY BREAD ALONE, BUT BY EVERY WORD THAT PROCEEDS FROM THE MOUTH OF GOD."
—*Deuteronomy 8:3*

was not as large a military presence there. However, people don't usually like being occupied, especially at spear point." And Strange makes it clear that Jesus never condemned the Romans or Herod Antipas (Herod the Great's son), though he did denounce people who were in league with the Romans.

Ironically, the most famous Jew who ever lived, from his lifetime to the present day, Jesus is not an important figure in Judaism. At the time he was known in the community by the Jewish Elders, who eventually turned him over to Pilate to be crucified. And he was famous across Judea for his enigmatic parables and his miracles. He also had a huge following by the time of his death: Some were people who expected a revolutionary to lead them in overthrowing the Romans; the majority respected him as a great rabbi. But in the end, Judaism does not consider Jesus as significant, and certainly not the Messiah, who they were (and still are) waiting for. ◆

Wine, bread, lamb, cheese and olive oil were probably the staples of Jesus' diet.

*Supper at Emmaus*
By Giovanni Francesco Barbieri
ca. 1626–29

Anna peers at Jesus being presented to Simeon.
Pictured: *Presentation of Jesus at the Temple*
By Pietro Antonio Novelli
1759

# JESUS IS BROUGHT TO THE TEMPLE

FOLLOWING THE REQUIREMENT FOR ALL JEWISH BOYS, THE INFANT
IS TAKEN TO JERUSALEM FOR A RITUAL EVENT.

LIKE ANY JEWISH MALE, ON THE EIGHTH DAY OF life, Jesus was circumcised and named, marking him as a member of the covenant people of Abraham, Isaac and Jacob, and securing for him privileges and obligations before God. The ritual would most likely have been performed by Joseph, although it could have been performed by the village rabbi.

Firstborn sons had an additional rite. Any time after the child's 31st day, he would be presented by his father to a priest and declared to be a first-born. The priest asked if the father would prefer to give his son as a priest or to redeem the boy for five shekels. After payment, the boy was redeemed, blessed, and returned to his father.

One can clearly picture the scene: Mary and Joseph would have walked from Bethlehem to Jeru-salem, joining the thousands of people who flowed through the temple precincts in Jerusalem each year. Endless rounds of sacrifices and ceremonies brought them there. But there was something about this couple and the child they brought that made them different from the others. Something about them caught the eye of two devoted worshippers. What could it be?

Simeon spotted Jesus first. Luke describes him as "just and devout." His faith went beyond outward conformity to Jewish law and created in him a heartfelt devotion to God. He spent much time in the temple. He is said to be influenced by the Holy Spirit on three occasions. Luke tells us he eagerly

> **"AFTER EIGHT DAYS HAD PASSED, IT WAS TIME TO CIRCUMCISE THE CHILD, HE WAS CALLED JESUS, THE NAME GIVEN BY THE ANGEL BEFORE HE WAS CONCEIVED IN THE WOMB."**
> —Luke 2:21

awaited "the Consolation (Comfort) of Israel." In this title are gathered all the promises and prophecies of the Messiah. Simeon lived in hopeful expectation of a Savior, Deliverer and King. Indeed, the Holy Spirit had impressed on his heart that he would not die until his eyes had beheld the Messiah.

When Mary, Joseph and Jesus join the flow of worshippers into the temple, something about them catches Simeon's eye. We are not told if he rushes to greet them, or how Mary and Joseph respond. Perhaps they spoke of their angelic visitations. Or of Jesus' birth in Bethlehem and the shepherds' story. Luke does say Simeon took the baby in his arms. In that instant, a lifetime of hoping and praying and meditating on the law and the prophets

## "*THERE WAS A MAN... WHOSE NAME WAS SIMEON; AND THE SAME MAN WAS JUST AND DEVOUT...AND THE HOLY GHOST WAS UPON HIM.*"

—*Luke 2:25*

flashed across his consciousness. In some inscrutable way, the Holy Spirit whispered to his spirit, "This is the One."

A song of praise gushes from Simeon's mouth, leaving Mary and Joseph once again in wonderment and awe. Simeon's praise is followed by a blessing, and then a difficult warning for Mary. He tell her of conflict to come. As miraculous as

this baby might be, Simeon warns, he will pierce his mother's soul.

Seemingly without a break, another spiritually minded elder approaches. Anna, the prophetess, is descended from the tribe of Asher. This would make her family residents of Galilee like Mary and Joseph. It may have been their manner of dress or speech or how they carried Jesus, but something drew Anna to them. Perhaps she overheard Simeon. Maybe she pieced together the biblical profile of a Galilean baby born not in Galilee but Bethlehem of Judea. It is equally likely that the Holy Spirit impressed a message on Anna's heart as he had done for Simeon.

There, in that bustling temple, Anna bursts forth into thanksgivings to God. We are not told how passersby responded or how the priests reacted. They had seen her there daily for years and would have known this was a special moment. Anna speaks, the Scriptures say, of Baby Jesus to all who looked for redemption in Jerusalem.

The ages-old countdown was complete. This one child fit the profile that was so clearly laid out in the Bible. Thousands of details, symbols, stories, and ceremonies came together when God became human that he might bring consolation and redemption to the whole world. They knew it was him, and they were glad. ◆

## { THE WISDOM OF ANNA }

Anna's Hebrew name, Hannah, means grace. She was a prophetess, implying a deep insight into both the Scriptures and the human heart, able to apply God's Word with directness and force under the influence of God's spirit.

She was of greatly advanced age. Scripture says she had been married for seven years and then widowed. Assuming a minimum marital age of 12, she would have been a widow by 19 at the earliest. Since then, she made a daily practice of fasting and praying in the temple for 84 years. This suggests she was at least 103 years of age when she met Jesus at the temple.

The circumcision of Jesus, about a week after his birth, was done in accordance with Jewish law.

*The Circumcision of Jesus Christ*
By Luca Signorelli
ca. 1490–91

When Jesus first calls his apostles, he challenges them to become fishers of men.

*The Calling of the First Apostles*
By Nikanor Grigoryevich Chernetsov
1866

# DID JESUS FOUND CHRISTIANITY?

HE NEVER WANTED TO START A NEW RELIGION;
HE JUST WANTED TO TRANSFORM JUDAISM.

IT'S SOMETIMES FORGOTTEN THAT JESUS NEVER renounced his Jewishness and never broke away from his religion; he died a Jew, and he didn't start Christianity before his death. It was his followers, over the centuries, who created the new religion. James Strange, PhD, doesn't believe Jesus was trying to reform Judaism completely, but rather was offering a contrarian voice. "He thinks some attitudes are wrong and some practices are wrong. He did want repentance; he wanted people to think about the pending Kingdom of God and change their behavior now before the Kingdom was fully present. He knew all their attitudes about each other and what they valued had to be changed, but that's all in the orbit of Judaism."

In other words, Jesus was not like the theologian Martin Luther, who wanted to revolutionize Christianity and the Roman Catholic Church when he nailed his Ninety-five Theses on a church door in 1517. Strange points out: "Jesus doesn't go about it in the same systematic way. I believe scholars who say any fight Jesus is having with Jewish leaders is an interfamily fight."

Paul V.M. Flesher, PhD, also points out that in the first part of the Synoptic Gospels (those of Matthew, Mark and Luke, which all relate similar stories), Jesus' message is more about emphasizing religious reform, trusting in God and moral purity more than anything else: "He is trying to change Galilean Judaism."

"I think the most important point about Jesus' life as a Jew is that he lived in Galilee, not Judea [Judea is where Jerusalem is located]," adds Flesher. "That is the Judaism he was familiar with; he clearly knew little about Judea, Jerusalem or temple worship and its vast support system. He lived a week's walk from Jerusalem. If Matthew, Mark and Luke are correct, the adult Jesus only visited Jerusalem at the end of his life."

> "[JESUS] WANTED PEOPLE TO THINK ABOUT THE PENDING KINGDOM OF GOD... BUT THAT'S ALL IN THE ORBIT OF JUDAISM."
> —James Strange, PhD

"His message changes as he gets closer to Judea. Perhaps there is more of a desire to overthrow this temple-based Judaism that he is discovering," Flesher says. "It is hard to tell in the material that purports to come from his last weeks or months of life how to separate his anger over religion from his anger over the politics of an occupied country." ◆

In John 4:10, Jesus tells the Samaritan woman:
"If you knew who it is that asks you for a drink, you
would have asked him and he would have given you
living water." He then explains that he is the Messiah.
Pictured: *Christ and the Samaritan Woman*
By Cornelis de Vos
1630

CHAPTER

5

*The World's
Greatest Teacher*

# THE WISDOM
## OF CHRIST

FOR 2,000 YEARS, THE INSPIRED TEACHINGS OF JESUS OF NAZARETH
HAVE HAD AN ENORMOUS IMPACT ON PEOPLE EVERYWHERE.
THEIR PROFOUND POWER HAS NEVER DIMINISHED.

NEW TESTAMENT HISTORY IS BASED MAINLY ON THE Gospels of Matthew, Mark, Luke and John; and the Epistles of St. Paul (who was not one of the original Twelve Apostles). Taken together, these accounts describe the three-year Ministry of Jesus, which include his teachings and his miracles.

Jesus clearly understood his audience. He was preaching mainly to humble, unsophisticated folk, so he spoke in humble, unsophisticated terms. His sermons often employed homespun parables, to which common people could relate. This gained their confidence; they could see that he was one of them. And the more they listened to him and heard stories about his teachings elsewhere and witnessed or heard about his miracles, the more he was considered a real prophet and possibly the real Messiah. That, of course, became very dangerous for Jesus, and ultimately led to his arrest and death on Good Friday.

St. Paul's Epistles to members of the early church make up a sizable proportion of the 27 books that constitute the New Testament. As many as 14 of the Epistles are generally considered to be authentic works, written or dictated by Paul himself. Others were presumably contributed by his contemporaries, or later authors writing in his style so the letters appear authentic.

There have been many generations of scrutiny, commentary and reverence for these lessons, the moral and spiritual precepts expressed by Jesus during his brief ministry. And while it's true that many of his ideas—such as The Golden Rule: ("Do unto others as you would have done unto you")—are foundational in other religions and philosophical systems, the sayings and actions of Jesus have a unique tone and clarity that make them so universal and enduring. Here are some of the most important.

### THE SERMON ON THE MOUNT

The Gospels do not record the name or exact location of the mountain where Jesus addressed his followers on that historic occasion. But the Sermon on the Mount is the longest, most comprehensive individual record of the spiritual and moral teachings of Jesus. One might consider it the "Master Sermon." It summarizes all the moral precepts of Jesus, as described in the Gospels of Matthew (4:13–25 and 5:1–29) and Luke (6:17–49).

This included the Beatitudes (Matthew 5:1–7:29), in which Jesus outlines the foundation of his societal ideals:

*When Jesus saw the crowds, he went up the mountain; and after he sat down, his Disciples came to him. Then he began to*

In the Sermon on the Mount, Jesus delivered the Beatitudes, which outline the central tenets of Christianity.

*The Sermon on the Mount*
By Charles Rolt
1861

When the crowd wants to stone the adulteress, Jesus tells them, "Let him who is without sin among you be the first to throw a stone."
Pictured: *The Woman Taken in Adultery*
Artist unknown
ca. 1860

*speak, and taught them, saying: "Blessed
are the poor in spirit, for theirs is the
kingdom of heaven. Blessed are those
who mourn, for they shall be comforted.
Blessed are the meek, for they shall inherit
the earth."*

Each of those first three Beatitudes addresses some condition of his followers: They were certainly mostly poor peasants; among them there surely must have been some who were mourning lost loved ones; and certainly all would have considered themselves meek, which didn't just mean "timid," but being of lowly station, as subjects of the unsympathetic Roman occupation.

These initial teachings reveal to us Jesus' ability to understand and show compassion for his flock. His obvious empathy certainly was more attractive than any fire-and-brimstone evangelical harangue, the meat and potatoes of any false prophet, then and now.

The subsequent Beatitudes deal with what Jesus considers the personal moral values he wishes to instill in his followers—and all of mankind.

In his view, it is proper for a soul to hunger and thirst for righteousness; to be merciful; to be pure in heart; to be a peacemaker; and to be patient when persecuted, reviled and falsely accused. It is holy to be peaceful and patient under difficult, sometimes even intolerable, circumstances, and to turn the other cheek when injured. This was a novel and unique development in the social philosophy and religious thinking of the day.

Among these moral values, the indispensable one is highlighted in St. Paul's First Letter to the Corinthians (13:13), in which he states:

*And now these three remain: Faith, Hope
and Love. But the greatest of these is Love.*

In this letter to members of the Christian community of Corinth, Paul reminds us Jesus preached the then unheard-of idea of loving one's enemies! This was revolutionary.

The Old Testament often shows us a vengeful, jealous, unforgiving God. In the Beatitudes, that image is revised by Jesus, who emphasizes God's loving and forgiving aspects, quite at variance with (for example) this passage from Exodus 20:5–6:

*He mocketh at us; His curse hath fallen
down upon us; His wrath will pursue us,
till He destroys us! For He, the Lord our
God, He is a jealous God, and He visiteth
all the fathers' sins on the children to the
third and the fourth generation of them
that hate Him.*

After that fearsome passage, it is noted that "His mercy on thousands fall," but the damage has already been done: The idea is deeply implanted that—if we sin—we should be fearful of God's vengeance upon ourselves, and even upon our descendants! This is a gloomy prospect indeed, which Jesus seeks to remedy with his promise of love, forgiveness and redemption.

### JESUS AND THE ADULTEROUS WOMAN

Unsurprisingly, there was sex in Biblical times. People were not very different 2,000 years ago. They were intelligent and had the same ambitions, fears, hopes, delights and foibles as we do today; they just lived in a simpler world. And of course, sexual attraction was just as strong then as now, even if first-century societies dealt with it differently, adhering to first-century customs.

So not surprisingly, Jesus was challenged about the punishment for adultery. In Matthew 5:27–29, Christ says:

*"You have heard that it was said, 'You
shall not commit adultery.' But I say to
you that everyone who looks at a woman
with lust has already committed adultery
with her in his heart. If your right eye
causes you to sin, tear it out and throw it
away. And if your right hand causes you
to sin, cut it off and throw it away; it is
better for you to lose one of your members
than for your whole body to go into hell."*

That seems quite severe. But on the other hand, in John 8:1–11, we find a gentler, more tolerant approach.

*The Miracle of the
Five Loaves and Two Fishes*
Artist unknown
ca. 1590

This lesson reminds us that, since none of us is perfect, it is nobler and more holy to be understanding, and to be merciful to one another.

Later, in Matthew 7:1–2, Christ says:

> *"Stop judging, that you may not be judged.
> For as you judge, so will you be judged,
> and the measure with which you measure
> will be measured out to you."*

## TURNING THE OTHER CHEEK

One of Jesus' most resonating, revelatory, and perhaps difficult teachings was his exhortation to resist revenge. As he says in Matthew 5:38–39:

> *"Ye have heard that it hath been said, 'An
> eye for an eye, and a tooth for a tooth.' But
> I say unto you, that ye resist not evil: but
> whosoever shall smite thee on thy right
> cheek, turn to him the other also."*

Jesus rejects the Old Testament incitement, almost obligation, to pursue revenge. He offers an alternative solution to violence—peaceful resistance. Mahatma Gandhi and Martin Luther King Jr. followed this philosophy and changed the world.

This teaching is also from the Sermon on the Mount, and expands upon the Beatitude "Blessed are the peacemakers, for they shall be called the children of God."

The day after his Mount of Olives sermon, Jesus was teaching in the temple when a group of Pharisees brought in a woman accused of adultery. The penalty prescribed by the laws of the time was stoning. Should they carry out the sentence? Jesus slyly suggested: "Whoever is without sin, let him cast the first stone."

The Pharisees backed away. Jesus, when alone with the woman, asked if she had been condemned by anyone. She had not. Jesus then said he would not condemn her either, and that she should go in peace and sin no more.

This policy of forgiveness is echoed in Matthew 6:14–15. He says:

> *"If you forgive others their transgressions,
> your heavenly Father will forgive you."*

## SERVING TWO MASTERS

In the Sermon on the Mount, as described in Matthew 6:24, comes the lesson that, "No man can serve two masters," or, as it appears in alternate versions, "No man can serve both God and mammon."

The latter interprets *mammon* as money, by extension the riches of the physical world. This serves to illustrate that there is no way to sincerely and adequately serve opposing interests.

In the words of Jesus as transcribed by Matthew in the King James Bible:

> *"No man can serve two masters: for either
> he will hate the one, and love the other; or
> else he will hold to the one, and despise the
> other, Ye cannot serve God and mammon."*

# { THE MIRACLE WORKER } Was there more to them than we think?

It would be presumptuous to think we could know what was in the mind of Jesus during the several stages of his ministry. But it is worth considering that his miracles, like his sermons and parables, may have also been teaching techniques.

For instance, the miracle of Jesus raising Lazarus from the dead could have been Jesus dramatically demonstrating, in our physical world, the abstract concept of resurrection that awaits all souls who come to God through him. Such a dramatic event would surely be an effective educational device.

Similarly, the converting of water into wine at the Marriage at Cana might be interpreted as an illustration of the mystery of the transubstantiation celebrated in the Mass. This might be seen as a physical world illustration of what is really an ineffable phenomenon.

One of Jesus' most famous miracles was healing the man blind from birth. The Apostles, believing blindness to be a punishment from God, ask Jesus whether it was the man himself, or his parents, who had sinned.

"Neither this man nor his parents sinned," said Jesus, "but this happened so that the works of God might be displayed in him" (John 9:1–12).

Then Jesus spits on the ground, bends down and makes a mud compress that he places on the man's eyes. Jesus tells him to go wash his eyes in a pool called Siloam (which means "sent," suggesting that Jesus is sent to deliver sight).

When the blind man returns, he can see. When other villagers ask him how, he explains that the man called Jesus had cured him. Unsure whether it is really the same man, or someone else, they asked one another, "Is that not the blind beggar?"

He is both. He inhabits the same body, but he is also a changed man because now he sees the light—both literally and spiritually.

*Raising of Lazarus*
By Giuseppe Porta
ca. 1540–45

*Jesus raises Lazarus from the dead, a metaphor for our spiritual resurrection through him.*

THE WORLD'S GREATEST TEACHER

The lesson? It is impossible to pursue material assets in the secular world without losing traction in the spiritual world. You cannot have one foot in the temple while the other foot is with the money-changer. We must commit to one or the other: either lay up temporary treasure in your counting house, or lay up eternal treasures in heaven.

## THE PRODIGAL SON

As told in Luke 15:11–32, this is the story of a father and his two sons. The younger one asks his father for his inheritance right away, instead of waiting until his father's passing. The father gives his son his share, after which the young man leaves and goes "abroad." He squanders the money and is subsequently reduced to working the lowest level subsistence jobs and eating the same swill given to the pigs. Luke recounts Jesus' parable:

*"And when he came to himself, he said,*
*'How many hired servants of my father's*
*have bread enough and to spare, and*
*I perish with hunger! I will arise and*
*go to my father, and will say unto him,*
*Father, I have sinned against heaven,*
*and before thee, and am no more worthy*
*to be called thy son: make me as one of*
*thy hired servants'. And he arose, and*
*came to his father. But when he was yet a*
*great way off, his father saw him, and had*
*compassion, and ran, and fell on his neck*
*and kissed him."*

His father forgives him unconditionally, welcomes him home and throws a sumptuous feast, telling his other son to kill the fattest calf for the meal.

The older brother—understandably—is resentful. He questions the affection lavished on his philandering brother when he, the good son, has remained faithful to his father and worked for him on the farm. "When did you ever kill the fattest calf for a feast for me?" he asks. But the father puts their lives in perspective and says, basically, when did you ever want for anything, wasn't I always here for you, and didn't I always give you my love? Your brother made

a mistake and paid for it dearly, and let's now rejoice, "for what was lost is found."

The father is clearly God, and the brothers represent sinners and the righteous, both of whom God loves equally, celebrating the return of one who he thought was lost forever.

## BELIEVING WITHOUT SEEING

According to the Gospel of John (20:24–29), after the crucifixion and resurrection, when the disciples told Thomas that they had seen the risen Jesus in the flesh, Thomas answered: "Unless I see the nail marks in his hands and put my finger where the nails were, and put my hand into his side, I will not believe it."

Presumably Thomas, although an Apostle, had never been truly convinced that Jesus was the Son of God. He clearly believed in the finality of death, that when you are dead you are dead—and that was as true for Jesus as for any other human.

Days later, when all the Apostles were gathered in a closed room, Jesus materialized before them. He greeted them, then asked Thomas to examine his hands, and to put his own hands into the wound in his side. Jesus then admonished his Apostle: "Do you believe now because you can see me? How happy are those who believe without seeing!"

The lesson here is that some things in life that are real, even when we don't—or can't—have direct sensory experience of them. We tend to put more trust in what our physical senses tell us, than what we can accept others tell us. We are more inclined to accept the mysteries of science than the mysteries of faith.

As another Thomas, the Italian Dominican friar and philosopher St. Thomas Aquinas (1225–1274), expressed this mystery: "Faith is not meant to replace reason, but is for those things reason cannot explain."

The notion of life after death has been with us all along. Some anthropologists theorize that belief in the afterlife originated in antiquity, when primitive men dreamed of people they had seen dead and buried. Dreams often seem real, so they assumed that their friends were visiting from some place in the afterlife where the dead lived on. ◆

# { JESUS AND THE ROMANS }
## Did Christ ever actually criticize them?

Jesus and his early followers probably had very little if any interaction with Romans, until, of course, Jesus was crucified. In the Gospels, there is no evidence of Jesus saying anything negative about the Romans. In fact, when a crowd tried to trick Jesus into denouncing paying taxes to the Romans, he firmly told them "render unto Caesar what is Caesar's, and unto God what belongs to God."

There is a story in the New Testament in which a Roman centurion approached Jesus because one of his soldiers was ill; he asked Jesus if he would heal the man. When Jesus offered to see the soldier, the centurion replied, "Lord, I do not deserve to have you come under my roof. But just say the word. And Jesus' response was, "Truly I tell you, I have not found anyone in Israel with such great faith."

In the centuries that followed Christ's crucifixion, eventually the Romans became predominantly Christian. In the fourth century, the Emperor Constantine, having converted to Christianity, declared all of the Roman Empire to be Christian, in order to unify all the various Christian factions.

*The Crucifixion*
*By Master of the Virgo Inter Virgines*
*ca. 1487*

*Longinus was a centurion who pierced Jesus' side, but was healed of his blindness when Christ's blood fell into his eyes.*

*The miracle of resurrection created a wave of shock and awe for all those who witnessed it.*

*Jesus Christ Raises the Son of the Widow of Nain*, from a 19th-century collection of biblical illustrations for children

# RAISING THE DEAD
## MIRACLES

IT IS PERHAPS THE ULTIMATE FEAT—BEING ABLE TO BRING LOVED ONES
BACK TO LIFE. AND JESUS USES HIS POWERS WISELY.

IN THE FIRST RECORDED RESURRECTION OF THE New Testament, Jesus has attracted a large crowd by his teachings and his miracles. One day, the crowd follows Jesus to a tiny town called Nain. As the excited multitude approaches the city, another group appears. Somber. Weeping and wailing. It is the funeral cortège of a young man, the only son of a widow. In biblical times, widows were easily identifiable by a special garb, though scholars are not certain of its appearance.

The contrast could not be greater. The nucleus of one group is a dead boy in a coffin. The nucleus of the other is the Creator of Life himself. The crowd of death exudes sorrow. The crowd of life radiates joy.

In one of the most dramatic scenes of the Bible, the two crowds collide.

The widow's grief was beyond description. She had already lost her husband. Now she is burying her only son—her last love—and with him, her only means of support. The awful power of death towered over her life and emotions.

When Jesus saw her, "He had compassion on her and said to her, 'Do not weep'" (Luke 7:13). A murmur must have rippled through the crowd. Why is he telling her not to weep? Look at her—she is utterly without hope. Of course she should weep.

Jesus approaches the young man's corpse. He was being carried on a bier, a litter, by his grieving friends. His body had been wrapped in grave clothes and anointed with spices. A hush falls over the scene.

Jesus lays his hands on the litter. He speaks. "Young man, I say to you, arise" (Luke 7:14).

Time stands still. What a moment! Every person there realizes the significance of his words. Death rules over all. It is the universal enemy. Undefeated and undefeatable. Just who is this carpenter from Nazareth?

With understated elegance, Luke says, "So he who was dead sat up and began to speak" (Luke 7:15). Tears of joy. Shouts of amazement. A rumble of wonder. What is this? Who is this?

> "HE SAID, 'YOUNG MAN, I SAY TO YOU, ARISE.' SO HE WHO WAS DEAD SAT UP AND BEGAN TO SPEAK."
>
> —Luke 7:14–15

Word spread like wildfire. A teacher unlike any other has arrived. His name is Jesus. In him, death has met its match. Wherever he goes, he finds sadness and death. Wherever he is received, he brings gladness and life.

Never in their wildest dreams could his followers have imagined that Jesus was only just getting warmed up.

## JESUS RAISES THE DAUGHTER OF A SYNAGOGUE LEADER

By now, Jesus is a sensation. Crowds press against him for even just a touch, hoping for their miracle. The pleas for help come in so fast, that his second recorded resurrection is interrupted, creating a story within a story.

A man named Jairus pushes through and falls at Jesus' feet. A buzz runs through the crowd. This man is the respected ruler of Capernaum's synagogue, yet he bows at the feet of an itinerant rabbi, begging earnestly, "My little daughter lies at the point of death. Come and lay Your hands on her, that she may be healed, and she will live" (Mark 5:23).

What did Jesus feel in that moment? Compassion? Sorrow? Peace? The Scriptures leave us to wonder, and Jesus accompanies Jairus without comment.

But the journey is interrupted. Jesus stops suddenly and looks around. "Who touched me?" he says.

He has been weaving his way through throngs of excited, happy, scared, desperate people. *Everybody* is touching him. The question seems silly, and his disciples say so.

But somebody touched Jesus with special intent, and he noticed. It was a touch of faith—the same faith that brought Jairus to Jesus. The same faith Jesus would summon people to all his life and his disciples would proclaim after him.

A woman, whose bleeding would not stop, believed in her heart that a touch from Jesus would make her whole. So she got close enough to touch the hem of his garment.

Immediately, Jesus felt "that power had gone out of him" (Mark 5:30). In his divine nature, the miracles of Jesus were simple things. But in his human nature, they were costly. They drained him.

"Who touched me?" Jesus asks.

The crowd waits.

## { THE SON OF A WIDOW }

The ancient port of Zarephath was made famous by the Jewish prophet Elijah almost 900 years before Jesus. Elijah met a widow when he first arrived, preparing her last morsel of food to share with her son. Elijah's ongoing miracle kept the impoverished family fed for a long time. There was joy in the widow's home.

But the difficulties of life come roaring back. The widow's son grew sick and "there was no breath left in him" (1 Kings 17:17). She lashes out at Elijah. He and his God, she says, are punishing her for some supposed guilt.

"Give me your son," the prophet says. He prays from the depths of his being. Elijah lays the corpse out and lays down on top of him, three times: Hand to hand, foot to foot, heart to heart. And he stretched himself out on the child three times, and cried out to the Lord and said, "O Lord my God, I pray, let this child's soul come back to him." Then the Lord heard the voice of Elijah; and the soul of the child came back to him, and he revived (1 Kings 17:21–22).

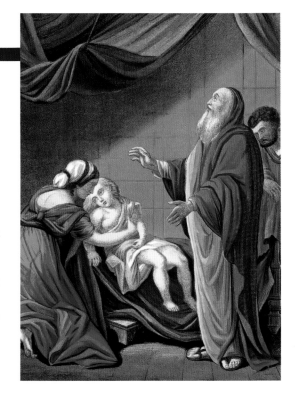

*Raising the Daughter of Jairus*
By James Tissot
1897

Jairus also waits. His panic grows by the moment, but what can he do? *Hurry, Jesus! Please! My daughter...*

The woman steps forward, fear written across her face. "I touched you," she says. Jesus calls her "Daughter" and says her faith has made her well. Jesus feels the same affection for the woman that Jairus feels for his daughter. There is nothing to fear. So ends the story within the story.

At that very moment, the larger story turns somber as messengers arrive with the heartbreaking news that Jairus' daughter is dead.

Why does God delay?

We can never know for sure. But could it be that for the Son of God the passage of time is never perceived as an emergency? He sees from the vantage point of eternity. He has all the time in the world. He possesses an infinity of it. Jesus looks at the brokenhearted father. "Do not be afraid,"

he says. "Only believe" (Mark 5:36). They continue on their way.

Jews had developed a specific method of mourning the dead. Professional wailers were hired to announce the sad occasion. Family and neighbors joined the raucous lament. Flute players added to the din (Matthew 9:23).

Jesus wades into the tumult. He calls for quiet. He announces that the child isn't dead but sleeping. The mourners ridicule him. They know death when they see it. They scoff at him.

Little do they realize the proclaimers of death are scoffing at death's living Lord.

Jesus enters the little girl's room. He comes alongside the weeping mother, takes the dead child's hand, and speaks. "Little girl, I say to you, arise" (Mark 5:41). And as simply as that, the 12-year-old girl "rose and walked." The mourners were wide-eyed and speechless.

*Jesus Raises Lazarus*
By Giotto
1305

## { KEEPING A SECRET }

Jesus often told exuberant followers to keep silent about him. After healing a leper, Jesus said, "See that you tell no one" (Matthew 8:4). After resurrecting Jairus' daughter, Jesus "charged [her parents] to tell no one what happened" (Luke 8:56). Why the secrecy? The most important clue comes from Mark's Gospel. After three disciples witnessed his glorious transfiguration, Jesus "commanded them that they should tell no one…till the Son of Man had risen from the dead" (Mark 9:9). Don't let the secret out until after the resurrection. Why? Because nobody really "gets" Jesus without understanding both his cross and resurrection too.

*Transfiguration of Christ*
By Giovanni Bellini
ca. 1478–79

And Jesus, always aware of what people really needed, told Jairus and his wife to give their daughter something to eat (Mark 5:43).

**JESUS CALLS FORTH A MUMMY**
The hamlet of Bethany sat on a hillside not far from Jerusalem. This pretty town is where Jesus enjoyed a homemade dinner with sisters Martha and Mary. He often resides here when ministering in Jerusalem. Later he will ascend to heaven from this place.

But for now Jesus is far away, continuing his ministry in a region "beyond the Jordan." He's keeping his distance from the mounting threats of the religious leaders in Jerusalem. Jesus receives word that his good friend Lazarus, Martha and Mary's brother, is sick. "Therefore the sisters sent to Him, saying, 'Lord, behold, he whom You love is sick'" (John 11:3). No doubt, they expect Jesus to drop everything and rush to Bethany to heal his friend.

But Jesus does the opposite. He waits—on purpose. "So, when He heard that he was sick, He stayed two more days in the place where He was" (John 11:6). There is nothing about Jesus that fits anybody's categories. He is his own man, with his own agenda, his own timing, and his own way of expressing his self-sacrificing love.

By the time they arrive in Bethany, Lazarus has been in the tomb four days. Jews considered this the day putrefaction set in. Mary is so distraught, she doesn't even come out to meet Jesus. Martha approaches with an accusation—"if you had been here, my brother would not have died"—and with faith—"but even now I know that whatever You ask of God, God will give You" (John 11:22).

Jesus answers with one of his most dramatic declarations: "I am the resurrection and the life. He who believes in Me, though he may die, he shall live" (John 11:25). Resurrection is not just his power, it is his identity. Furthermore, it is his promise to all who believe in him.

A large crowd has assembled at Lazarus's tomb. Mary finally arrives. Seeing the pain written across her face, Jesus wept. In a minipreview of his own resurrection to come, Jesus commands that the

# { THE MIRACLE SON }

The second resurrection of the Old Testament places Elijah's disciple Elisha in the spotlight. Elijah's earthly sojourn ends with a miracle, as "a chariot of fire appeared with horses of fire…and Elijah went up by a whirlwind into heaven" (2 Kings 2:11). Elisha witnesses this as proof that human life transcends earthly existence.

The stories of God's intervention and laws are etched across Elisha's imagination. He develops a ministry teaching God's truth and raising another generation of prophets to do the same. Along his regular route lay the village of Shunem. A wealthy woman there persuaded her husband to build a small apartment for Elisha. Elisha discovers she is childless but wants to be a mother. He promises she will soon embrace a son. The miracle comes true, and as often as Elisha visited, he sees the boy's growth.

But tragedy strikes. In a painful scene, the boy is in the fields when he cries out, "My head! My head!" and dies in his mother's arms (2 Kings 4:19). The Shunammite woman would not give up. She lays her son on Elisha's bed, saddles a donkey, and races 20 miles to Carmel to fetch the prophet. He offers to send his servant and staff. She insists Elisha come himself. When he arrives, Elisha follows his mentor's example. He lays himself over the boy. Warmth returns to the boy's body. He sneezes seven times and opens his eyes. Elisha summons the mother and says, "Pick up your son" (2 Kings 4:36).

stone over the tomb be removed. Martha protests because, using the archaic language, "by this time he stinketh" (John 11:39). Jesus insists. The people comply. Jesus prays and then cries out with a loud voice, "Lazarus, come forth!"

And he who had died came out bound hand and foot with grave-clothes, and his face was wrapped with a cloth. Jesus said to them, "Loose him, and let him go" (John 11:44).

Only Jesus can unwind death's grief and restore true happiness and joy.

Some believed. Some explained it away. From that day on, the religious leaders plotted to kill him (John 11:53). But Jesus has already proven both that the grave has no power over him and that God can use death to bring about grace and glory the world never saw coming.

### THE GRAVES GOD OPENS

It was his trip to resurrect Lazarus that brought Jesus back to the precincts of Jerusalem, where the religious leaders were planning to kill him. Soon, temple police would arrest Jesus and Roman soldiers would nail him to that old, rugged cross.

In Jerusalem's magnificent temple hung a veil that separated the innermost sanctum, called the Holy of Holies, from the larger chamber, called the Holy Place. Inside the veil rested the Ark of the Covenant, the most potent symbol of the presence, holiness, purity, and love of God on Earth.

The veil itself was a wonder. Sixty feet tall, 30 feet wide, and 4 inches thick, it was embroidered with angels in scarlet, purple and blue. This awe-inspiring veil stood as a stark reminder of the impenetrable separation between a holy God and an unholy people. It represented the barrier of sin and its consequences.

But the moment Jesus died, God marked the event with rapid-fire miracles. The Earth shook. Rocks split open. The darkness that had shrouded the crucifixion was lifted. To cap it off, the massive veil in the temple was suddenly ripped in two, from top to bottom.

## { A PROPHET'S BONES }

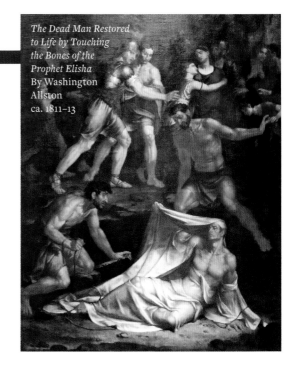

*The Dead Man Restored to Life by Touching the Bones of the Prophet Elisha* By Washington Allston ca. 1811–13

In one of the strangest resurrections recorded in Scripture, an unnamed man has died. While being carried to his burial, a band of Moabite raiders appears. In their haste to hide themselves, the man's friends cast his corpse into an open grave. It turns out to be the grave of the prophet Elisha. The fresh corpse, which has presumably been wrapped for burial, rolls until it touches the prophet's bones.

Elisha's story is full of miracles. He healed leprosy, caused an iron ax-head to float, and multiplied bread to feed an army. He purified water and kept a supply of oil flowing for a widow. He raised the son of the woman of Shunem from the dead.

Now, unnamed pallbearers throw an unnamed corpse into the tomb of Elisha, and "when the man was let down and touched the bones of Elisha, he revived and stood on his feet." (2 Kings 13:21)

*The Crucifixion of Christ*
By Giusto de' Menabuoi
Late 1300s

No human hand could have done this. Only God. What Jesus accomplished in his death and resurrection opened the way for morally fallen people to enter the presence of God. The barrier was gone. Now, all who believed could come, just as they were. Jesus did the impossible. He opened the way to God. It was his sacrifice, his work, his payment and his grace.

As if to enact a living parable of the significance of Christ's death, God layered on yet another wonder: "And the graves were opened; and many bodies of the saints who had fallen asleep were raised; and coming out of the graves after His resurrection, they went into the holy city and appeared to many" (Matthew 27:52–53).

A more accurate translation would read: "And, having come out of the graves, after his resurrection, they went into the holy city and appeared unto many." At the moment Jesus died, God performed multiple resurrections, as if to shout to the universe that Jesus' death brings life. We cannot say who these revived corpses were, except to say they were "saints," meaning believers in the one true and living God, the Creator. Their number was "many."

These were mothers, fathers, sisters, brothers and children. They had been mourned and buried, but they were now suddenly back from the dead. Imagine the reunions—the widening of the eyes, the disbelieving exclamations, the squeals of delight and the tearful embraces.

Imagine the whispers about Jesus.

The curse of death is broken. It is broken spiritually in the torn veil. It is broken physically in the open graves. In Jesus Christ, crucified and risen again, that old enemy called death has finally met its match. The death of Jesus is truly the death of death itself. ◆

There are many sacred books that purport to tell of Jesus' time on Earth and his message, besides the ones in the "official" Bible.

HYMNS
ANCIENT & MODERN
REVISED
1950

OLY BIBLE
&
APOCRYPHA

# JESUS IN THE
## APOCRYPHA

THESE LONG-DISPUTED GOSPELS WERE LEFT OUT OF THE SACRED CANON, BUT DOES THAT MEAN THE STORIES IN THEM—INCLUDING JESUS KILLING HIS PLAYMATES AND GETTING MARRIED—ARE UNTRUE?

THE APOCRYPHA ARE DISPARATE TEXTS AND WRITings, most thought to have been written at around the same time as the four Gospels included in the New Testament, but which weren't selected to be in the "official" Bible. They were determined not to be valid, or acceptable, accounts of Jesus' life, by the church. They have been points of contention for centuries, and remain so.

The word *Apocrypha* comes from the Medieval Latin word *apocryphus*, meaning "secret or noncanonical," which comes from the Greek *apókryphos*, meaning "hidden" or "obscure." We've worn down the modern word to mean "unlikely to have happened," which is fine by the church, which took that position about one and a half millennia ago.

There's a school of thought that maintains that just because the Catholic Church didn't like the cut of the cloth of some of these writings, particularly the Gospel of Judas and the Infancy Gospels, doesn't mean that they aren't true.

"In Christian history, when what emerged as the mainstream church was deciding what books they valued, they started to use the term *apókryphos* for books that they didn't," says Tony Burke, PhD, a professor of early Christianity at York University in Toronto, and one of North America's leading Apocrypha experts.

The story of Jesus was preserved orally for almost 100 years before being put into writing. It wasn't until the fourth century that the canon, meaning the texts that are officially considered part of the Bible, was established. "The ones that did end up in there all have a certain uniform doctrine," explains Burke. "They fit together theologically. This is as the church developed and they thought about what ideas they liked, what they didn't."

In the Bible, there are no details of Jesus' life between the Holy Family's flight into Egypt and when he was 30, other than the pilgrimage to the

## THE STORY OF JESUS WAS PRESERVED ORALLY FOR ALMOST 100 YEARS BEFORE BEING PUT INTO WRITING.

temple in Jerusalem with his parents when he was 12. But apocryphal portrayals of Jesus fill in some of the blanks. For example, the Infancy Gospel of Thomas describes Jesus as a child (see page 75). Some parts of this text portray him benevolently, but others paint him as a spoiled and impatient prince. And we're being nice—the Infancy Gospel depicts a malevolent supernatural brat: When another child accidentally bumps into him in the market, the text has Jesus striking him dead without warning. He curses another child to wither and die, which the boy promptly does. Jesus also causes his teacher to have a breakdown, the text quoting the poor fellow: "I strove to get me a disciple and I am found to have a master." In other spots, Jesus blinds those who question him.

Other stories from the Infancy Gospel are more in character, including resurrections, curing the sick and blessing Joseph's wheat crop.

Over the centuries, the idea of Jesus having a wife became taboo, but it crops up in some of the Apocrypha. In the Gospel of Philip, Mary Magdalene is described as Jesus' companion, which some interpret as wife. But Catholic authorities preferred

# "JESUS SAID TO THEM, 'MY WIFE...SHE IS ABLE TO BE MY DISCIPLE.'"
—*Gospel of Jesus' Wife*

to keep him chaste, and away from their version of temptation. Burke says: "It's likely Jesus could have been married. The fact that the authors of the New Testament Gospels don't mention it, it's really because it's just not part of what they're interested in saying. They also don't say that Jesus went to the bathroom, but obviously he did."

In 2012, a 1,200-year-old document called the Gospel of Jesus' Wife was discovered. While most of it was destroyed, this ambiguous line remains: "The Disciples said to Jesus.... Mary is [not?] worthy of it.... Jesus said to them, 'My wife...she is able to be my Disciple.'" This caused great controversy, as you'd expect, and is generally not considered genuine. (While this is the only one to mention Jesus' wife, the Gospel of Philip references Jesus kissing Mary Magdalene on the mouth.)

"It's mostly a modern interest because the church, as it developed, were all monastics," notes Burke. "They weren't interested in presenting a Jesus who was married. If anything, they want to present a

Jesus who was not. They want to present a Jesus like them, who was an ascetic and a monastic and without sin. If monastics think about sex as sinful, they want Jesus to be without sin. Modern readers have pulled away from those kinds of things, and they're interested in a Jesus who's much more like themselves." In the Gospel of Thomas (not to be confused with the Infancy Gospel of Thomas), someone questions Mary Magdalene's worthiness as a follower because she is a woman. According to the text, Jesus says:

*"Behold, I shall lead her, that I may make her male, in order that she also may become a living spirit like you males. For every woman who makes herself male shall enter into the kingdom of heaven."*

This would imply that Jesus believed women and men are equal, as do many of his interactions with women in the Bible, but here it presents the quixotic dilemma of whether that equality requires a gender transformation!

Also, Mary Magdalene was never a prostitute—and nowhere does the Bible assert she was. This notion came later, manufactured by the church to keep women out of the clergy.

In the apocryphal Gospel of Mary, Magdalene is portrayed as very close to Jesus, and even guides his incredibly lost disciples after his crucifixion. And according to this account, she is visited by him after his death.

And the noncanonical book, Apocalypse of Peter is a brochure of what hell is like: Apparently it's everlasting impalement and being hung by your tongue. We're actually surprised that one didn't get in.

The Revelation of the Magi is an eighth-century text that presents the Three Wise Men quite differently. In this story, the birth of Christ is a prophecy passed down between generations of the Magi. They wait lifetimes for the star to guide them to Jesus (who is supposed to be their savior). "Jesus is the star. It's not a sign of where Jesus is that they follow, but he is actually the star itself, and they follow this star until it comes to Bethlehem and then the star becomes Jesus as a human being," says Burke. ◆

Marriage at Cana
By Garofalo
1531

For Jesus' first miracle, the Marriage at Cana, he turned water into wine.

# { DID JESUS EVER CONDEMN DRINKING OR HOMOSEXUALITY? } Short answer: No.

We have all been given the impression that the Bible condemns drinking, homosexuality and many other things. And it's true, the Old Testament can be pretty damning. But did Jesus himself ever speak out against these things?

There are no overt references to Jesus partaking in a glass of wine, but, like other Judeans of his time, he probably drank daily. Of course, there are several passages in the Bible that denounce drunkenness, but drinking in moderation was universally common, and would not have been an obstacle to holiness.

The Israeli historian Magen Broshi devoted a whole chapter of his book, *Bread, Wine, Walls and Scrolls*, to wine in Biblical times. Broshi concluded that wine was abundant throughout the region. In biblical passages dealing with the produce of ancient Palestine, he noted that grapes were one of the main crops. Wine is mentioned in the Bible 141 times, and Scripture is supported by the archaeological findings of thousands of wine presses. Given how ubiquitous wine was, it would be unlikely that Jesus would abstain.

Wine was substantially different in those days. It was often spiced with herbs, sometimes sweetened with lead, and always diluted with water. Broshi said that drinkers would use ratios ranging from one part wine for one part water, to one part wine for three parts water, which, no doubt, helped dilute the lead.

So Jesus and his disciples probably drank in moderation, following the instruction of Proverbs 23:20: "Do not join those who drink too much wine or gorge themselves on meat, for drunkards and gluttons become poor."

As for homosexuality, Jesus never actually spoke against it. The closest he gets to condemning sexual practices is his admonishment of adultery and divorce. (He is very clear in his disapproval of those.) Still, many contemporary conservative Christians have long demonized same-sex relations as a terrible sin, and the Old Testament *is* unambiguous in its condemnation of them. But the Bible, especially the Old Testament,

was written partly to set laws and societal norms for those unenlightened times.

Chris Ayers, pastor of Wedgewood Baptist Church in Charlotte, North Carolina, says this condemnation is a result of a strict—and selective—reading of the Bible. He points out that, yes, there are passages condemning homosexuality, but they are much more violent and vile than any Christian would surely support. (Leviticus 20:13 for instance says that anyone who commits a homosexual act should be killed, which is, thankfully, not the prevailing sentiment today.)

But Jesus himself never disavowed homosexuality, though he surely would have come across it in his travels. Instead, he was supportive of love and loving thy neighbor without exceptions.

This is perfectly summed up by Innocent Himbaza, PhD, a biblical scholar at the University of Fribourg, in his book *The Bible on the Question of Homosexuality*: "Problems can arise when we want to find in the Bible answers to specific questions raised by the society in which we live. We risk making the Bible say what it does not."

Himbaza and his colleagues note that for every instance of homophobia, there are Bible passages that speak about love for others, like Leviticus 19:17:

> You shall not hate your brother in your heart, but you shall reason frankly with your neighbor, lest you incur sin because of him.

Ayers goes on to say that even Jesus was selective in what he believed in the Bible. "Plastered throughout the Old Testament is the idea that if you are good, God is going to bless you real good, and that includes financial blessings. If you are bad, well, bad things are going to happen to you. But when you come to Jesus, he says the rain falls on who? The just. Well, they knew that. But Jesus goes on to say that the rain also falls on the unjust. With that one statement Jesus wiped out a large chunk of the Bible. And in that same passage when Jesus said love your enemy, Jesus also wiped out a huge portion of the Old Testament. All that killing they thought was the will of God was not the will of God."

OPTIMAM PARTEM ELEGIT

Like many who lived in ancient Palestine, Jesus likely partook of wine on a daily basis as part of his meals.

Christ in the House of Martha and Mary
By Alessandro Allori
1605

123

When Jesus was fasting in the Judean desert, Satan appears to him and tries to tempt him toward sin.

The Temptation of Christ
in the Wilderness
By Juan de Flandes
ca. 1500

# MAJOR PLAYERS IN
## JESUS' LIFE

THE LIFE OF JESUS IS SPRINKLED WITH HUMAN, ANGELIC AND DEMONIC
INTERACTIONS, EACH ONE REVEALING SOMETHING OF GOD'S GLORIOUS PLAN.

### THE PHARISEES

The Pharisees are a perennial thorn in Jesus' side. Partly a political powerhouse but mainly a theological enforcement agency, the sect of the Pharisees is intensely dedicated to purifying Judaism. They take upon themselves the task of ensuring the laws of the rabbis are followed to the letter.

When Jesus comes on the scene, they don't know what to make of him. He is a Jew and seems to endorse Judaism; but at the same time, he presents a different view of Judaism. The Pharisees hound his every step and parse his every syllable to find occasion to charge Jesus with theological crimes.

Jesus denounces them, calling them "a brood of vipers" and "hypocrites." He says they are "sons of hell," "blind guides" and "an evil and adulterous generation." He accuses them of setting their own rules, called "traditions," that they add to the inspired Law of Moses. The Pharisees relentlessly agitate against Jesus, and for their self-righteous hypocrisy, rank among the Bible's premier villains.

### SATAN AND DEMONS

Christ's life is sprinkled with regular encounters with the dark side. When he launches his ministry, he is tempted by Satan with magnificent allurements. Though weakened and famished, Jesus overcomes each temptation by citing the Word of God.

Jesus routinely casts out demons from afflicted people. On one occasion, he delivers a man who lived among tombs and was considered beyond redemption. Once the "legion" of demons is cast out, this formerly hopeless maniac is found in his right mind, sitting with Jesus and conversing. The demonic legion, however, has entered a herd of swine, which promptly runs off a cliff into the sea and perishes (Matthew 8:30–34).

Jesus battles these dark forces incessantly. For their cruelty, rebellion, hatred of God and barbarism against people, these sinister agencies find their place at the top of the heap of scriptural villains.

### MARY MAGDALENE

Mary Magdalene is often confused with the notorious "sinner" who anointed Jesus' feet with her tears and dried them with her hair, though this has no foundation in fact. Others confuse her with Mary, the sister of Lazarus and Martha, which is, again, unfounded.

She appears for the first time in Luke 8:2, where she possesses enough wealth to sustain the ministry of Jesus and his disciples. Her motive is gratitude: Jesus has delivered Mary Magdalene from seven demons, and her life has been set free.

She remains loyal to Jesus from that point onward. Even when the other disciples flee from his crucifixion, Mary Magdalene remains until the bitter end.

She is there when the body of Jesus is laid in the grave. She returns with Salome and another Mary to anoint his body with spices. She is the first person to whom Jesus shows himself after his resurrection. Any supposed scandal between her and Jesus is a gross fiction, without any basis in fact whatsoever.

Mary Magdalene shines as a hero of faith, and she is one of the many significant women among the believers in Jesus.

### PONTIUS PILATE

Pilate was the Roman governor of Judea, the province that encompassed Jerusalem. That meant he was head of the judicial system, so when the Pharisees want to have Jesus executed, they need his stamp of approval. Jesus is charged with instigating riots throughout Galilee, calling himself the king of the Jews and interfering with the payment of taxes to Caesar. While Pilate is deciding the case, his wife sends him a message: "Don't have anything to do with that innocent man, for I have suffered a great deal today in a dream because of him" (Matthew 27:19). Pilate declares he finds "no fault in this man" (Luke 23:4); hoping to extricate himself from the entire affair; he sends Jesus' case to Herod Antipas, who is governor of Galilee, Jesus' home province, and therefore under Herod's jurisdiction. Herod, who is spending Passover in Jerusalem, asks Jesus if he's king of the Jews, and demands that he perform a miracle, but Jesus remains silent. To mock him, Herod has dressed Jesus in royal robes and sends him back to Pilate, for he, too, wants to avoid involvement in this controversial case.

Pilate again argues he can find no legal grounds to justify the execution of Jesus. Following a custom of the time, Pilate offers the crowd a choice: Set Jesus free or let a notorious traitor and murderer named Barabbas go. "Give us Barabbas!" the crowd cries. To appease them, Pilate has Jesus scourged, beaten and crowned with thorns. This still does not satisfy the mob, who shout, "Crucify him!" Seeing there is no placating them, Pilate "took water and washed his hands in front of the crowd [saying] 'I am innocent of this man's blood'" (Matthew 27:24). He orders Jesus to be flogged, then hands him over to be crucified. For knowing the course of justice and refusing it, Pilate rises to the fore as a coward and villain of the highest rank, in history and in Scripture. ◆

*Jesus Condemned by the Sanhedrin*
By Martin Schongauer
Late 15th century

*WHEN JESUS COMES ON THE SCENE, THEY DON'T KNOW WHAT TO MAKE OF HIM. HE IS A JEW AND SEEMS TO ENDORSE JUDAISM; BUT AT THE SAME TIME, HE PLACES HIMSELF ABOVE JUDAISM. THE PHARISEES HOUND HIS EVERY STEP AND PARSE HIS EVERY SYLLABLE TO FIND OCCASION TO CHARGE JESUS WITH THEOLOGICAL CRIMES.*

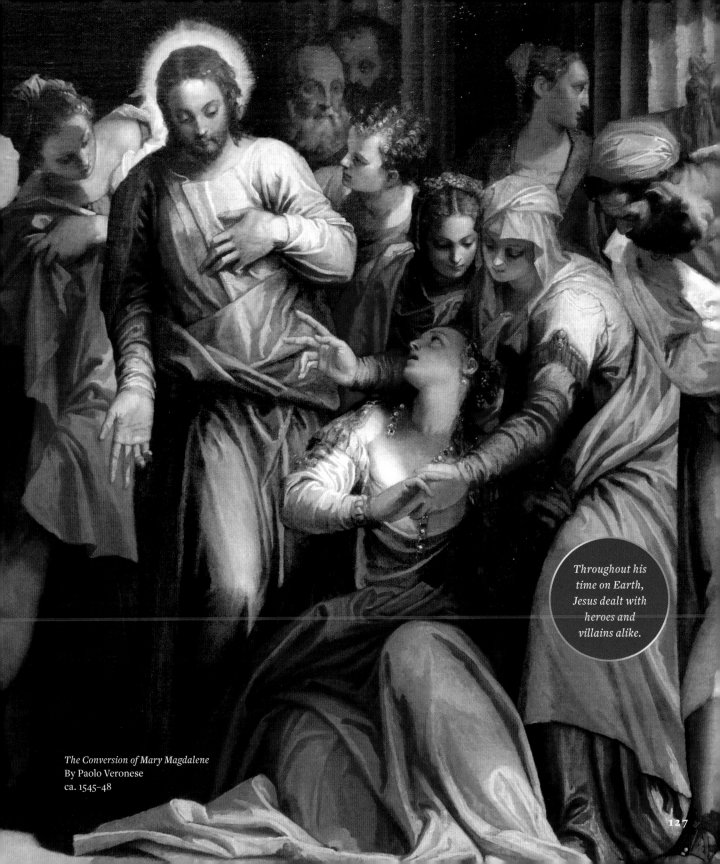

*The Conversion of Mary Magdalene*
By Paolo Veronese
ca. 1545–48

Throughout his time on Earth, Jesus dealt with heroes and villains alike.

**PERCEPTION** vs. **REALITY**

# WHAT DID
# JESUS LOOK LIKE?

### DESPITE HIS FAME, NOBODY ACTUALLY KNOWS.

IT IS PRETTY CERTAIN THAT IN REAL LIFE, JESUS OF Nazareth did not look like he does in the paintings featured in this book.

Almost all of these depictions were images created by Europeans or Westerners. And most of us see Jesus as we see ourselves: Caucasian, traditionally handsome and admirably tall. Some conjectures put him at around 5-foot-9 (based on well…nothing!). The Bible, though, never mentions Jesus as tall, or of average height, and not once describes his facial features, the color of his eyes or the length of his hair. But to us Jesus is basically a good-looking, free-spirited, California surfer dude-1960s hippie.

## "HIS HEAD AND HIS HAIRS WERE WHITE LIKE WOOL, AS WHITE AS SNOW…"
—*Revelation 1:14–15*

So how did this happen? The Gospel writers likely weren't interested in conveying Christ's looks—they weren't important. Jesus' message, teachings, suffering, death and triumphant Resurrection were what concerned the New Testament authors.

Secondly, the writers may not have known Jesus, or spoken to anyone who ever saw him in person, even though there is an outside chance that Matthew and John were actual disciples. The New Testament writers were recording oral history, which reasonably could have included physical descriptions of the Son of God. The fact that there are none in the New Testament—nor any in the Apocrypha—presumably indicates Jesus' appearance was consciously thought to be irrelevant.

Jesus is not universally portrayed as white and blue-eyed, though. In African churches, he is often depicted with black skin. And he is more Mediterranean and ascetic-looking in the Greek and other Orthodox churches. But because Christianity started with his Jewish followers and was ultimately organized by the Romans and spread across Europe, European painters created a Christ for the sensibilities and needs of their time, not Christ's.

The likelihood is that Jesus would have had the darker skin of the Semites and been shorter than we think of him—he would have stood out as an alien if he looked the way we commonly visualize him! A research group in England a few years ago came up with a 3D image of the head of Christ by applying the principles of the new field of science known as forensic anthropology to skulls from Judea in the first century, and concluded that Jesus would have had dark skin, a thick nose, widely spaced brown eyes, short, tightly curled black hair, and a coarse black beard. (In their rendering, he almost looks Neanderthal.)

The truth, of course, is that if we believe Jesus is God, then he is perfect and would have looked beatific to whoever beheld him, which is, frankly, more or less the impression we get of him from the Bible. ◆

In parts of Africa, Jesus is depicted as black, as in this painting The Madonna and Child of Soweto, displayed in a South African church.

The saddest crown ever worn:
Jesus' crown of thorns was put
on his head by Roman soldiers
to mock the King of the Jews.

CHAPTER

# 6

*The Passion of Christ*

Once his work on Earth was completed and his human form was finally shed, Jesus ascended into heaven.

The Ascension
By Gustave Doré
1879

# DID JESUS
## DIE FOR OUR SINS?

THE MOST IMPORTANT AND TRANSFORMATIVE EVENT IN
JESUS' LIFE, AND IN CHRISTIANITY, IS CLOAKED IN MYSTERY.
WHY DID HE HAVE TO DIE TO FULFILL HIS EARTHLY MISSION,
AND HAVE WE EVEN UNDERSTOOD IT CORRECTLY?

THAT CHRIST DIED FOR OUR SINS IS THE FUNDAMENtal assertion of Christianity. It is the basic kerygma, or proclaimed message, from the earliest times to the one we hear from church pulpits and street corner preachers today. Yet, there are some very cogent reasons that this should not be so.

Most importantly, from a historical and theological perspective, there has not been a clear and concise agreement about what the statement even means from the very beginning of Christianity.

Who is Christ, and why did he have to die? How did it work? Was it a deal? A necessity? Who was involved? In the early centuries, a commonly held theory was that it was a ransom paid, but to whom? To God the Father? Some even proposed it was paid to the devil, who held us prisoner in sin and death.

The most popular, and unfortunately, most damaging interpretation came from St. Anselm in the 11th century, in his *Cur Deus Homo* (or "Why God Become Man"). Working within his feudal framework, he reasoned that if the lord of the manor (the God of Creation) has been offended by his serf (humankind), then fitting and proper restitution must be paid. St. Anselm thought he was showcasing God's mercy by explaining that the Father had arranged for just such an atonement: The reparation had to come from the serf, but since the lord's dignity was paramount and beyond the serf's capacity, someone with the lord's own level of dignity was needed to repair the offense. The brilliant compromise: someone who was both Son of God and Son of Man!

It was a short step from an offended God to an angry God, already so often portrayed in the Hebrew Scriptures, and since the aggrieved party was so lofty, only death would put things right. In other words, God demanded the bloody sacrifice of his only son in order not to be furiously angry with us anymore. Search the wounded psyches of thousands of generations of Christians and you will see evidence of this.

This heinous notion rode roughshod over the next centuries, beyond any distinctions between Catholic or Protestant, and became the "penal substitution theory": Humankind needed to be severely punished for its transgression in the Garden of Eden, so the innocent Jesus would substitute himself to undergo the lightning bolts of God's righteous anger in our stead. Christ died for our sins, indeed! How could we not be grateful—and frightened and ashamed?

FORTUNATELY, IN OUR TIME, SPIRITUAL WRITERS like Franciscan friar Richard Rohr, and theologians like Sister Elizabeth Johnson, PhD, professor emerita

## { THE LAST SUPPER }
### What really happened?

All three Synoptic Gospels present the Last Supper as a Passover meal, and with good reason. Christ and his followers had come to Jerusalem to celebrate the solemn Jewish feast of the Passover, and, in a foundational belief of Christianity, Jesus is our Passover (1 Corinthians 5), and the cup of wine he and the apostles shared becomes the blood of a New Covenant.

Nonetheless, many question if it was a Passover meal at all. Part of the discrepancy arises because of John's Gospel, in which Jesus is portrayed as crucified on the

## *"THIS IS MY BODY GIVEN FOR YOU; DO THIS IN REMEMBRANCE OF ME."*
—*Luke 22:19*

Day of Preparation, when the lamb was slaughtered for the Passover. This signifies Jesus as the new Lamb of God. This tradition endured in the liturgical worship of both Eastern and Western Christianity, where Good Friday is officially called *Parasceve*, or "Preparation" in Greek. Theologically, it was necessary that it be a Passover supper, and it might have been so historically, but we do not know that for certain.

The Gospels mention only an intimate gathering with Jesus and his apostles. Jesus speaks few words at the supper, but they are momentous and stupendous: "This is my Body, given for you!" (Paul reports this also in 1 Corinthians 11.) For more than a thousand years (after which a guy named Berengarius questioned what became known as the "Real Presence," and then, a few centuries later, came the Protestant Reformation), Jesus was taken at his word. As one Eucharistic hymn put it: The Word made Flesh made Bread Flesh with a Word! And, if the Risen Christ really "fills the universe in all its parts" ("all in all," Ephesians 1:23), then surely he can "fill" a bit of bread!

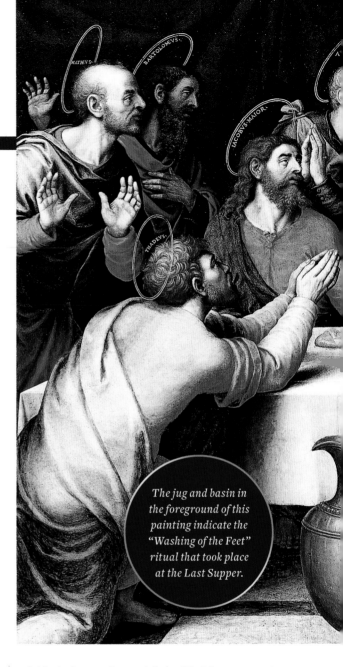

*The jug and basin in the foreground of this painting indicate the "Washing of the Feet" ritual that took place at the Last Supper.*

Intriguingly, some have pointed out that Jesus may have been pointing to the apostles; when he said, "This is My Body," he may have meant them. This is also fine and accurate, since, through sharing in the One Bread, we also become One Body—his, as Paul explains in the same letter (1 Corinthians 10 and 12).

Jesus pronounces considerably more words in John's version of the meal, but the Last Supper discourse (John

*The Last Supper*
By Juan de Juanes
ca. 1555–62

13–17), like much else in John, is better understood as his post-resurrection reflections to his disciples, or as their meditations and experiences of Jesus up until this last Gospel was written at the end of the first century.

In any case, John has no institution of the Eucharist. What he does have, however, is the sublime Washing of the Feet, still commemorated on Holy Thursday. Thus the day is often called Maundy Thursday, from *Mandatum*, or "commandment" in Latin: from Christ's command to the Apostles "that you also do as I have done to you" (John 13:15). Some have wondered why the Washing of Feet is not a major sacrament. Many believe Christianity would have been immeasurably better off and authentic had believers regularly engaged in such a humbling and inspiring ritual, perhaps pouring oil, like Mary of Bethany did, over one another's feet.   —*Father Michael K. Holleran*

This 15th-century painting depicts the "T"-shaped cross often used by the Romans, not the lowercase "t" shape we usually see.

*The Crucifixion*
By Gerard David
ca. 1475

of theology at Fordham University, have confronted this conception head on. In particular, in her recent book *Creation and the Cross*, Johnson outlines starkly and persuasively what the inevitable consequences are of this understanding of the Christian mystery.

First of all, the penal theory creates a false and disastrous image of God. He is an irascible, violent father who requires blood sacrifice and death from his only son. How has this not fatally poisoned countless minds and hearts, and seeded fear and violence in human history over the centuries? Of course, other scriptural passages that could counteract this portrait were ignored, often willfully, to preserve this destructive and utterly untenable image of God.

In this view, the natural world is neglected and mistreated with impunity. There is no ecological concern where we are seen as part of nature, but only as dominators who act out against its backdrop. And, as Johnson notes with concern, there is a whole history of animal sacrifice in the worship of God that is completely unacceptable today. Sacrifice is so entrenched in our imaginations and liturgical language, without adequate qualification and explanation, that one almost despairs of ever escaping.

So, is there a way out? Is there a perspective that respects the message and tradition, but can extricate us from these deadly quicksands? As Rohr points out, in the 14th century Franciscan theologian John Duns Scotus proposed an alternative orthodoxy: that the Incarnation of the Son in Jesus Christ was not a begrudging Plan B on God's part. On the contrary: It was God's original intention.

The Universe was created in Christ and geared to Him. God so loved the world (John 3:16) that he wanted a more intimate solidarity, actually to become part of Creation, in Christ, who, Rohr says, "emptied himself" of divine privilege to become one of us.

God wanted, through Christ, to share our own life, to taste what it is like to be created and human, and to give us a taste of what it is like to share Divine Life. For God, it was entirely and eternally a work of love. There is no other motive, no other matrix, no other atmosphere, and no other goal. As Rohr states so beautifully: God loves things by becoming them.

SO NOW WE ARE FINALLY IN A POSITION TO APPROACH the cross and see it authentically, perhaps with surprisingly new eyes. The proposition is startling, subversive and inescapable: There was no need for Jesus to die to placate an angry God, a God who already madly and helplessly loved us from all eternity.

As Rohr says, Christ did not come to change God's mind about us, but to change our mind about God.

Who then is this God? One who, in Jesus, would be in such close and embracing solidarity with us that he would even share our death, infusing it and curing it, with his own presence and divine life. In unflinching unity with us, he would plunge into the very depths of our darkness and despair, and indeed, into our sin, and bear them up in his mercy and forgiveness.

He would be so courageously close to our sin that he would take the worst humanity has to offer, an

> ## "FORGIVE THEM, FATHER, FOR THEY KNOW NOT WHAT THEY DO."
> —*Luke 23:34*

unimaginably cruel and unjust death, such as we often inflict on one another, and still hold it in forgiveness and love. There is nothing so reprehensible that we humans can dream that is not swallowed up in this torrent of Divine Mercy. Not even the killing of God himself—which is not the deed of "the Jews," as we so perversely and complacently claimed for centuries, but the reaction of all of us when faced with the revelation of who God is and what he demands of us in this world: unstinting, uncalculating, unbounded and unconditional love for absolutely everyone always.

So the conclusion is also inescapable: God may not have wanted the crucifixion; but we did! It's no wonder we killed him! And yet, no wonder he used it as an astounding and unsuspected vehicle for his mercy and love.

In that sense, Christ did need to "die": not to placate a bloodthirsty Father, but to placate us, in that we could be assured that not even wickedness, not even death, is an ultimate or insurmountable threat, but is included in the arms of God's mercy. And just as death sums up and encapsulates the value and meaning of a human life, so Jesus' death, in complete trust—"Into your hands I commend my spirit" (Luke 23:46), his last words before dying—and limitless forgiveness, sums up and consummates his own life, and offers us the promise, potential and plenitude of eternal life in him.

So, yes, he died "for our sins," but also to liberate us from death! The cross illustrates, as the modern philosopher René Girard maintains, that scapegoating is the primary defensive mechanism of human "civilization": demonizing and destroying something or someone "other, out there," rather than facing our own demons and limitations.

Jesus is also saying to us, as Rohr poignantly suggests: I am what you do to yourselves, what you cannot accept in yourselves. Now you have permission, gazing upon me, not to fear what makes you feel most unworthy, weak or ashamed, including your sins. In a most reassuring sense, Jesus takes upon himself all our weakness and sin, as traditionally claimed.

THIS NEW VISION OF JESUS' TIME ON EARTH MEANS we must also revisit the meaning of Holy Saturday, of Jesus' mysterious day in the tomb, of his "descent into hell," the underworld (Hades, Sheol), as affirmed in the Apostles' Creed.

Medieval theology asserted that when Jesus' body was in the tomb, his soul descended to "hell," and his divinity, while everywhere, was the link that remained united to both body and soul. But what transpires is not a "touchdown dance" (Rohr's words) of Jesus, but a "Harrowing of Hell": Jesus shatters the gates and bars of the underworld, and brings up those who died before him, beginning with Adam and Eve, whom he is depicted as taking by the hand and escorting from prison to paradise. Such an interim realm was called *Limbus Patrum*, or "Limbo of the Fathers," since the patriarchs and kings of the Old Testament reputedly had to wait for Jesus to open the gates of paradise by his own passage.

This is symbolic and pictorial, for the actual reality and dimension of Jesus' solidarity is even more astonishing. As the Jesuit theologian Ladislaus Boros asserts, borrowing a phrase from Jesus himself about Jonah and the whale, Jesus entered the very depths of reality, the void, the black hole at the heart of creation, which Jesus calls the "Heart of the Earth." ("The Son of Man will be three days and three nights in the heart of the earth." Matthew 12:40) Thus, in that interim moment and liminal space of Holy Saturday, descending to the very root of the world, the humanity of Jesus begins to expand to the very dimensions of the cosmos, in a way that will be fully manifest and potent the morning of the resurrection.

Some theologians, most famously Hans Urs von Balthasar, suggest that this moment was one of impenetrable darkness, as Jesus continued to experience the wrath of the father's countenance upon the sins of all humankind that he bore; but I hope I have dismantled and discredited such a view, since God is only love. More truly, as the main prayer for Holy Saturday affirms in the Carthusian monastic liturgy: "With tranquil heart, let us await his triumph, already illumined with a wholly new light." Already dawning is the light and promise of the Resurrection. In that mystery, Christ's solidarity with creation will reach its most sublime expression and expansion.

For now, though, will we have the courage to face the stunning reality that Christianity has misrepresented its basic message? After 2,000 years, we are still in our infancy!

Finally, the empty tomb and slightly conflicting accounts of Easter morning simply reflect historical distance, and the astonishment of the early Christ-following community. Some have suggested that, had someone actually been present with a video camera at the moment of resurrection, they would only have caught a blazing flash of light. Because Jesus' resurrected body was not the resuscitation of a corpse, but his radiating out into the universe, beyond all previous limits of space and time, to become "All in All"! —*Father Michael K. Holleran*

There is no historical record of Pontius Pilate releasing anyone at Passover.

*Jesus in Front of Pontius Pilate*
By Jan Joest van Kalkar
Date unknown

PERCEPTION VS. REALITY

# DID JESUS FALL THREE TIMES ON THE WAY TO CALVARY?

IT'S ONE OF THE MOST ICONIC IMAGES OF CHRIST. BUT STRANGELY,
IT'S NOT MENTIONED IN ANY OF THE GOSPELS. SO WHERE DID IT COME FROM?

PERHAPS NO EVENT IN JESUS' LIFE, OTHER THAN his crucifixion itself, is more painful, sad or profoundly human than his falling under the weight of the cross he would soon be nailed to and die on. It is burned into the consciousness of Christians from our earliest religious education. In fact, perhaps it is sadder and more painful, because we know the crucifixion leads to his return to God and eternal glory, and we believe that means our own salvation.

But the horror of carrying the impossibly heavy instrument of your own death and falling multiple times to the ground, exhausted, and having to get up again and continue, is something we can all imagine; we can all relate to that sense of powerlessness.

On that journey, not only is Christ most indelibly us, but we are most indelibly him, crushed under the burden of our imperfectly led lives and manifold disappointments, irrevocably journeying to our end.

The Bible, however, mentions none of that. All four Gospels cover Christ's passion and crucifixion, and Mark and Luke in particular provide many details. But in none of the accounts does Jesus fall or struggle; Mark in particular refers to Jesus being helped by Simon of Cyrene, a North African from what would now be Libya: "And they led Him out to crucify Him. And they pressed into service a passer-by coming from the country, Simon of Cyrene (the father of Alexander and Rufus), to bear his Cross" (Mark 15:20–21).

The story of Christ falling three times appears almost 1,700 years later, when St. Leonard of Porto Maurizio, an Italian, formalized what we today know as the 14 Stations of the Cross, a ritual devotion that grew out of the more informal pilgrimages believers made to Jerusalem for centuries, during which they retraced Christ's last steps on the Via Dolorosa, believed to be his route to Calvary. Two Stations (5 and 8) relate to events told in the Bible—Simon being drafted to help Jesus carry the cross, and Jesus admonishing the weeping women of Jerusalem. The other stations are mostly symbolic. There is no mention in the Bible of Veronica (Station 6) who comes out of the crowd to offer Jesus a cloth to wipe his face, and who, according to the legend, received the cloth back from Jesus, with the image of his face on it. The Veil of Veronica, as it is known, is preserved in St. Peter's Basilica in the Vatican. And the Bible does not recount Station 4, when Jesus' mother, Mary, comes up to touch him and cries in pain for him.

It is likely, however, that Jesus would have fallen under the weight of his cross. Whatever the actual shape—some speculate it was an *X*, the commonly used *T*, or the symmetrical vertical and horizontal beams that we know as the cross—he was basically carrying a tree trunk, and he had been profusely tortured before embarking. Just because the Bible doesn't say it happened doesn't mean it didn't. ◆

Images of Christ collapsing under the weight of the cross are common in Christian art.

*Christ Falling on the Way to Calvary*
By Raphael
ca. 1514–16

*Christ Carrying the Cross*
By Bernardino Luini
ca. 1520

# THE CRUCIFIXION AND BURIAL OF JESUS

### EVERYTHING JESUS SUFFERED WAS NECESSARY FOR THE REDEMPTION OF THE MORALLY BROKEN OBJECTS OF GOD'S ETERNAL AFFECTION.

WHAT THE BIBLE DESCRIBES IN FOUR STARK WORDS— "and they crucified him"—would have been traumatic to behold and an unspeakable horror to endure. The Persians are credited with inventing this torture and the Romans with perfecting it. Jews repudiated this form of execution, another factor that made it difficult for many to accept Jesus as their Messiah.

St. Paul declares, "Christ died for our sins" (1 Corinthians 15:3). Two words represent history: "Christ died," a physical, literal, visible moment in time, attested by a host of eyewitnesses. Anyone who was there could have seen it. Three words represent theology: "for our sins," the invisible meaning, purpose, and effect of his death. This detail would not have been apparent to eyewitnesses—it had to be revealed by God in his word and communicated by his disciples to the world.

The physiological cruelties of death by crucifixion have been detailed by modern medicine. The scene is graphic and difficult to consider.

Jesus was arrested by temple soldiers and underwent a series of illegal trials in front of Jewish leaders, before being handed over to Roman officials. During these, he was beaten across his head and face, stripped, mocked and spit upon. The Roman governor, Pilate, handed Jesus over for scourging (John 19:1). This was a form of torture in itself, in that Jesus was tied to a pole and beaten with a whip until the skin on his back and chest was shredded, often exposing muscle and bone. The crown of thorns, usually depicted as a ringlet encircling the head, more likely resembled a cap with thorns as hard as nails. This was pounded into Jesus' skull with a cudgel, causing pain beyond description (Mark 15:19).

If he was God, why did he not stop the agony?

The scriptural answer is simple: because of love. Everything Jesus did was necessary for the redemption of the morally broken objects of eternal affection—a world of lost sinners in need of a savior.

As Jesus is led to his death, he is required to carry his own cross. Weakened by the assaults he has already faced, another man carries it for him. He was crucified on a hill called Golgotha, an Aramaic word meaning the skull. The Latin equivalent has come into the English language as Calvary. There, on Mount Calvary, cruel hands laid him on an old rugged cross and thick spikes were driven through his hands and feet to hold him on it.

A sign was affixed to the top of the cross. Later artistic depictions often show the letters INRI, Latin initials for the phrase "Jesus of Nazareth, King of the Jews." It is a profound irony that what was meant as a statement of ridicule would turn out to declare such an indelible truth. Soldiers lifted the cross, set it in a hole, and stood back to guard the scene.

Researchers are uncertain as to the precise cause of death for a victim of crucifixion. It would have been virtually impossible to breathe without pressing up on one's feet. But the nails through the feet made that an excruciating act. After a few moments, victims would slump back down, putting the weight of the body on the nails through the wrists. The pattern of pressing up to gasp for air and slumping down for relief would have gone on for hours and sometimes days. A combination of blood loss, shock and asphyxiation would have hastened the victim's demise. To hurry up death, Roman soldiers often broke the victim's legs with a hammer, rendering it impossible to push up for air. By the time they came to do this to Jesus, he had already died.

Of the cries of Jesus from the cross, three rise to the fore. Known as the Word of Dereliction, Jesus said, "My God, my God, why have you forsaken me?" (Matthew 27:46). The apostles would say it was the consequence of Jesus bearing all the sins of human-kind, and with them, the divine condemnation so richly deserved. This mysterious breach in the eternal fellowship was the judgment of God falling on the sacrificial Lamb of God to redeem the people of God.

About three hours later, Jesus declares his Word of Triumph: "It is finished!" (John 19:30). The payment for sin was complete. The redemption price was paid in full by the shed blood of Christ. Divine justice was satisfied, and reconciliation between fallen human and a holy God was fully and finally effected. The apostles would teach Jesus' death was substitution-ary—one dying for another. Christ died for our sins.

In their minds, there has never been a Savior like Jesus and there has never been a love like Calvary.

In his final cry, the Word of Reunion, Jesus said, "Father, into your hands I commit my spirit" (Luke 23:46). Jesus announced his own death. He was nobody's victim. In that moment, his spirit and soul departed his body and went directly into the presence of the Most High. The impenetrable mystery of a breach in the divine fellowship was ended. Jesus had died. A soldier thrust a spear into his side to confirm the death.

When his soul and spirit departed his body, there was one believing thief whose soul and spirit went with him.

### PREPARATION FOR BURIAL

A member of the Jewish ruling council named Joseph of Arimathea offered his grave for the body of Jesus (Mark 19:38). Because the Sabbath was approaching, haste was required. It would have been a horrible curse to leave his body exposed on a holy day. So they wrapped him in a clean shroud and laid him in a typical tomb of the day—one of many caves carved into rock.

It would remain for his friends to finish his anoint-ing for burial after the Sabbath, but something remarkable happened before they ever got there. ◆

## { SIGNS OF MOURNING }

Death brought the community together in dramatic expressions of grief. These actions were considered demonstrations of honor for the deceased. They included: wailing or screaming or hiring professional wailers, beating the breast or other parts of the body, singing songs of lamentation, ripping apart one's garment, plucking out hairs from the head or beard, dressing in sackcloth (a burlap-like cloth used for making bags), blasting horns and wearing black. Cultural standards required passersby to join in the lament. Mourning might continue for a week for family members and a month for a ruler or king.

Vases filled with perfume for the dead were often found in Roman burials.

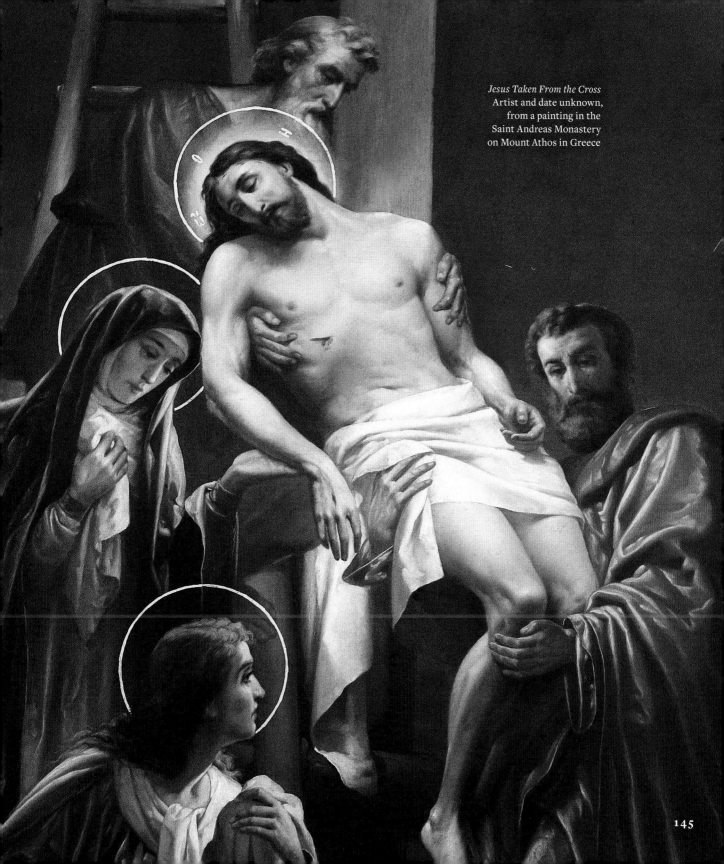

*Jesus Taken From the Cross*
Artist and date unknown,
from a painting in the
Saint Andreas Monastery
on Mount Athos in Greece

145

# BURIAL PRACTICES
# IN THE TIME OF CHRIST

ENTOMBING THE DEAD IMMEDIATELY WAS CRUCIAL IN JUDEA AT THE TIME OF
JESUS' DEATH, BUT THE EXECUTED WERE LESS SENSITIVELY TREATED.

AFTER JESUS WAS CRUCIFIED, HE WAS CERTAINLY quickly buried. In the book, *The Jewish War*, Craig Evans, PhD, professor of Christian origins at Houston Baptist University, cites Roman historian Josephus, who was writing around A.D. 75 "[Josephus] flat out states the Jews are so careful about funeral rights, even malefactors who have been sentenced to crucifixion are taken down and buried before sunset," he writes. "The dead were buried right away, wrapped in a cloth—embalming and cremation were not practiced—within a day after death." A year later, their bones were gathered up and placed in a niche or bone box. "They'd take chalk or charcoal or scratch in the limestone and write, *Esther lies Here* [so] when they go back one year later to collect the bones, they know who it is."

If Jesus' body and those of the two robbers crucified with him were not taken down and properly buried, on the eve of Passover no less, this would be a scandal and a profanation—a defilement of the Holy Land.

Evans notes that while some say Roman law did not permit crucified people to be buried, he maintains this is incorrect. Book 48, Chapter 24 of the "Digest of Justinian," a collection of Roman law assembled by Justinian in the sixth century, states that if the relatives of the person executed request the body, it should not be denied to them. And Josephus wrote that the Romans were able to maintain peace (as much as they did) because they allowed the Jewish people to observe their customs.

Of course, there were crucified people who were not buried because people didn't request their body: They were runaway slaves or highway robbers; they had committed high treason; they had attempted to assassinate Caesar; or they'd led an insurrection. "Their bodies might be crucified and burial denied, but that was the exception, not the rule," Evans says. Those corpses went into mass graves.

After Jesus was crucified, Scripture says that Joseph of Arimathea, a member of the Jewish high court, the Sanhedrin, went to Pontius Pilate and requested the body. Joseph buried Jesus in his own tomb, which by contemporary custom made it a place of dishonor because it had held an executed person. That was quite a sacrifice on Joseph's part, says Evans. However, "the people who hated Jesus and wanted him buried in dishonor would have objected and said, 'you have to put the body of an executed criminal in a tomb that has executed criminals in it.'"

In the days immediately after the crucifixion, the disciples hid, fearing arrest. The women, however, were safe. The earliest they could return was Sunday morning—Saturday was Shabbat, plus it was Passover. When they arrived, they found the tomb open and the body gone. Evans speculates the women probably assumed Jesus had been taken to where criminals are buried. But as we know from Scripture, whatever they may have feared was allayed when an angel told them that Jesus had risen from the dead. The rest, as they say, is history. ◆

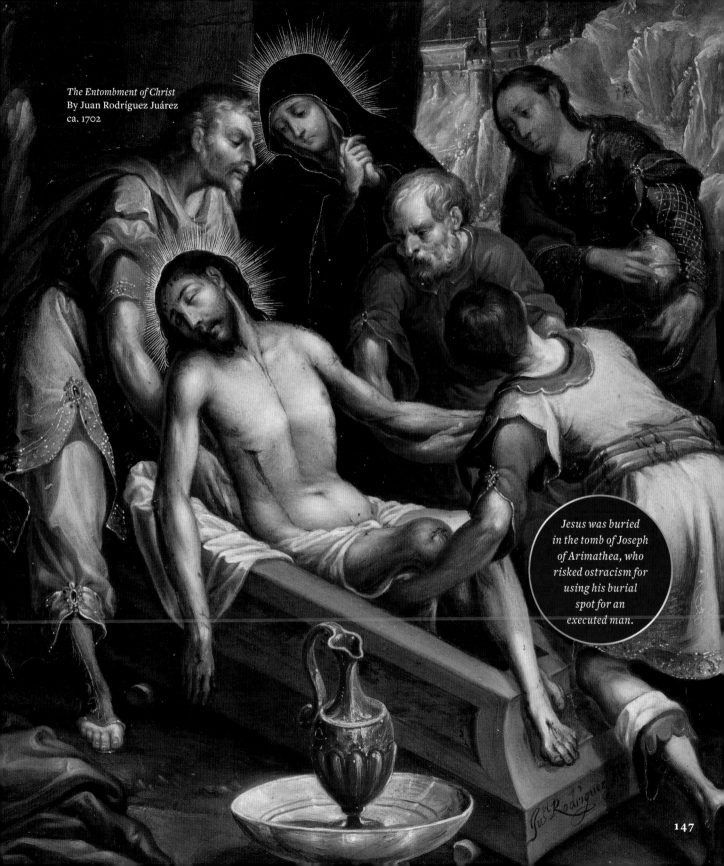

*The Entombment of Christ*
By Juan Rodríguez Juárez
ca. 1702

Jesus was buried in the tomb of Joseph of Arimathea, who risked ostracism for using his burial spot for an executed man.

147

The gravestone
is overturned.
The guards will
flee as the suffering
of Good Friday is
eclipsed by the Glory
of Resurrection
Sunday.

# WHY DIDN'T THE
## ROMANS GUARD
## THE TOMB?

THE GLORY OF JESUS' RESURRECTION UPENDED ANY ATTEMPT TO
PAINT THE DISCIPLES AS THIEVES WHO COULD DUPE THE SOLDIERS.

MATTHEW'S GOSPEL EXPLAINS THAT A STONE WAS rolled in front to seal the tomb. Archaeologists have unearthed a handful of such stones, weighing several hundred pounds, usually signifying a wealthy owner. Once in place, the stone was sealed. This would consist of a rope across the stone, held in place on each end by clay, impressed with the seal of Rome. Though it would have been an easy act, it also would have been a capital crime to break the seal.

At the request of Jewish leaders, a detachment of Roman guards was deployed at the tomb of Jesus. The Jews feared his disciples might steal the body, in an attempt to manufacture rumors of a resurrection (Matthew 27:62–66). The fact of the guards indicates that both Jewish and Roman authorities were familiar with the promises of Jesus' resurrection, and knew the implications if even a rumor got started.

It is inconceivable to think that highly efficient Roman guards would have failed at their duty. Had the disciples come to break the seal, roll away the stone, and steal the body, they would have stopped them. They stood duty day and night. They were not allowed even to lean against a rock, lest they fall asleep. A guard who fell asleep was often set on fire by a superior officer to wake him up. They took their jobs with all seriousness. The failure of their commission would have resulted in death.

The scriptural report is unmistakable in its claim:

*And behold, there was a great earthquake; for an angel of the Lord descended from heaven, and came and rolled back the stone from the door, and sat on it. His countenance was like lightning, and his clothing as white as snow. And the guards shook for fear of him, and became like dead men (Matthew 28:2–4).*

These same guards would later find themselves in the uncomfortable position of reporting the missing body of Jesus.

> ## "AN ANGEL OF THE LORD…ROLLED BACK THE STONE FROM THE DOOR."
> —*Matthew 28:2*

Rather than go to the Roman governor, they went to the chief priests who bribed them with "a large sum of money" to say the disciples stole the body while they slept. They also promised to protect the guards from retribution by Roman officials. Though this is the story that went out, it's unlikely that the dispirited disciples could mount such an operation right under the eyes of the well-oiled Roman military machine. ◆

# THE DAY OF
## THE RESURRECTION

THE STONE WAS ROLLED AWAY, THE GUARDS HAD SCATTERED, AND
THE TOMB WAS EMPTY. WHERE WAS JESUS?

THE TOMB WAS EMPTY. THIS SIMPLE CLAIM HAS CAP-
tivated the attention of believers and skeptics alike.
How do we account for the empty tomb of Jesus?

For people of faith, the answer is not difficult. Christ has been raised from the dead by the
miraculous power of God. To think that the same
omnipotent God, who created all things from nothing by the Word, could raise his only begotten Son
from the dead is a totally logical deduction.

The disciples have been downcast. Scattered.
Despondent. The One who stirred their imaginations with hope for a better life and an incredible

## THE WRITERS OF SCRIPTURE REVEL IN THE UNFOLDING DRAMA OF THE GREATEST STORY EVER TOLD.

eternity is dead and buried. The boot of Rome still
sits on the neck of the Jews. The weight of religion
and law still stoops the most ardent person of faith.
When Jesus died, hope died too.

Or so they imagined.

Then, a day dawned. By Jewish reckoning, it was
the third day from Friday's horrific crucifixion.

The first people to see the empty tomb were women.
Mary Magdalene, accompanied by others, had come
early in the morning to finish anointing the body of
Jesus. Sorrowing and heartbroken, they made their
way outside the city gates to the place where Jesus
lay. When they arrived, the scene before them must
have seemed surreal.

The stone was rolled away, the guards had scattered, and the tomb was empty. Later, they would
hear it was an earthquake that scared them away.
Where was Jesus?

The promise of his resurrection had scarcely
penetrated their minds, so at most there would only
be the faintest glimmer of hope. Could it be?

Suddenly, the rush is on.

Mary Magdalene, seeing the open tomb, runs to
Jerusalem. She finds Peter and John and announces
her findings. Not knowing what to believe, they race
toward the empty tomb. Meanwhile, the women who
had accompanied Mary enter the tomb. An angel
speaks to them, sending them to find the other disciples in order to inform them that Jesus has risen
again, and to instruct them to head to Galilee.

John outruns Peter, looks inside the tomb without entering, and sees the linen grave cloths lying
there. He doesn't know what to think. Peter catches
up and rushes right into the tomb. He sees the grave
cloths and the linen head cloth. John believes—
Jesus is alive! They race home.

For believers, it is not difficult to conceive that Jesus has risen and appears to his disciples in his human form.

*The Risen Christ*
By Marco Basaiti
ca. 1520

*Noli Me Tangere*
By Titian
ca. 1514

Meanwhile, Mary Magdalene has caught up and sits outside the tomb, weeping. Two angels speak to her. She turns around, and who should be standing there but Jesus himself.

Back in Jerusalem, Peter and John arrive home. The other women who saw the empty tomb give instructions to head to Galilee. Suddenly Mary Magdalene returns, exclaiming she has seen Jesus!

At the same time, the guards report to the chief priests what has happened. They conspire to bury the story. Word spreads. Two disciples travel on foot to a town called Emmaus. Along the way, Jesus meets them. Not recognizing him, they blurt out all the news about Jesus and his missing body. Finally, it dawns on them who he is and they are elated.

In Jerusalem, the disciples have hastily gathered. Jesus appears to Peter alone, then to the remaining disciples except for Thomas, and finally to Thomas. Appearances multiply until everybody is talking about it. The writers of Scripture revel in the unfolding drama of the greatest story every told. There is no room for any conclusion but that the epic redemption has culminated in a Risen Savior. Nothing is impossible with God. ◆

## { WHERE DID JESUS GO DURING HIS DAYS IN THE GRAVE? }

The Scriptures are clear that the body of Jesus was laid in the tomb. By his own testimony, however, his spirit and soul went to a place called Paradise. A Jewish historian, writing shortly after the days of Jesus to explain Judaism to gentiles, explained that Jews equated Paradise with a place called Abraham's Bosom. Jesus would later speak of Abraham's Bosom in the parable of the Rich Man and Lazarus (Luke 16:22).

All of these "compartments" were viewed as part of the place called Hades, the abode of the dead. When the Apostles' Creed affirms that Jesus, after his death, descended to hell; it is a reference to Paradise, not to the fires of divine condemnation.

Opinions diverge as to what Jesus did during that time. One interpretation suggests that Jesus made a victorious proclamation to his demonic foes, announcing that he was about to burst the bonds of the grave, break the power of death, and rise again (2 Peter 3:18, 19; 2:4).

As part of that victory, some scholars interpret Ephesians 4:8 to say that Christ led a triumphant procession of all the redeemed of ages past to their permanent home in heaven. He has truly fulfilled his identity as "the firstfruits of those who slept." Now, when people die, they wing their flight directly to heaven to be with God forever.

*Christ in the Realm of the Dead*
By Joakim Skovgaard
ca. 1891–94

Caves were often used as tombs.

# THE MOMENT OF THE
## RESURRECTION

THE SAME PERSON WHO TAUGHT, LOVED, SERVED AND WORKED
MIRACLES, ROSE AGAIN—LITERALLY AND PHYSICALLY.

TO ZERO IN ON THE PRECISE MOMENT OF THE RES-urrection of Jesus is to enter the realm of mystery. The storytellers are content to unfold the account through the eyes of disciples, guards, priests and the multitudes, without detailing what happened in the tomb. It is possible, however, to piece together a tentative scenario from God's Word.

### HIS BODY WAS RECONSTITUTED
The scriptural idea of resurrection creates a direct link between a person's pre- and post-resurrection body. For example, Saint Paul reveals that the "mortal" and "corruptible" aspect of our being—in context, the human body—will put on "incorruption" and "immortality" (1 Corinthians 15:54). In some mystical manner, Jesus' physical body was reconstituted in the very moment that he rose up from the grave. His followers recognized him. They knew him. They looked into his eyes and saw the scars on his hands, feet and side. The same body that was laid in the tomb after being crucified emerged from it as well.

### HIS BODY WAS GLORIFIED

As Jesus' body was reconstituted, it was also elevated. Though Jesus is morally perfect, his body was subject to the ravages and pains of Earth. This vulnerability was erased in the resurrection. Scripture affirms "the body is sown in corruption, it is raised in incorruption" (1 Corinthians 15:42). Saint Paul calls it "his glorious body" and says our "lowly body" will one day be like his (Philippians 3:21). The resurrection body of Jesus was his former body, reconstituted, glorified, and outfitted for eternity. In this resurrection body, Jesus rose up into a cloud (Acts 1:9), appeared in a room in which the doors were locked (John 20:26), sat on his heavenly throne (Revelation 5:13), and will one day return in the clouds to end history as we know it (Matthew 25:31).

### HIS SOUL AND SPIRIT WERE REUNITED WITH HIS BODY

With his material aspect now reconstituted and glorified, Jesus' immaterial aspect—his spirit and soul—now return to reanimate his body. Jesus is alive! He has risen from the dead. He is back. The same person who taught, loved, served and worked miracles, rose again—literally and physically.

### OTHER WONDERS OCCURRED

Christ's resurrection was accompanied by angels, the defeat of demons, an earthquake, the stone rolling away, the emergence of Jesus from his grave cloths, and his exit from the tomb. It only remains for us "to wait for His Son from heaven, whom He raised from the dead" (1 Thessalonians 1:10). ◆

# { THEORIES OF THE RESURRECTION }

Over the years, various alternative theories have arisen to explain the claim of the empty tomb.

•**The Swoon Theory** suggests Jesus did not really die; he simply passed out. This is hard to imagine given the efficiency of the Roman killing machine. Furthermore, the detail of "blood and water" flowing from his wounded side demonstrates the certainty of his death (John 19:34).

•**The Hallucination Theory** claims those who saw Jesus after his death were hallucinating, again a difficult premise considering that more than 500 people saw him at once (1 Corinthians 15:6).

•**The Vision Theory** says that Jesus arose spiritually, but not physically, from the dead. His appearances were more like apparitions. Again, this view is untenable, given the physicality of Christ's appearances—Jesus' eating, Mary's embrace and Thomas' touch (Luke 24:43, John 20:27).

•**The Theft Theory** maintains the disciples stole his body to fabricate a resurrection. This is virtually impossible given the heightened concern of the authorities over this potentiality, coupled with the despondency of the disciples.

•**The Legend Theory** suggests the whole story of Jesus belongs to the realm of legend, not history. This cannot account for the rise of the early church, the sudden courage of the disciples, and the willingness of the earliest Christians to be martyred for their faith in a Risen King.

All of these theories share the same common factor: a premise that denies the agency of God. In a world where God reigns, nothing is impossible, not even resurrection.

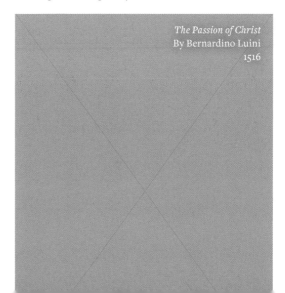

*The Passion of Christ*
By Bernardino Luini
1516

*Word of the resurrection spread from person to person, rather than in one divine burst of glory.*

*The Incredulity of Saint Thomas.*
*By Bartholomäus Bruyn*
*(Barthel Bruyn the Elder)*
*16th century*

# DISCOVERY
# OF THE BODY

THOUGH GOD IS PERFECTLY CAPABLE OF OVERWHELMING THE SENSES,
THIS IS NOT HIS NORMAL WAY OF COMMUNICATING HIS GOOD NEWS.

THE WRITERS OF SCRIPTURE ALLOW THE DISCOVERY of the momentous occasion to unfold. The first people to know something big was happening were the Roman guards when the Angel of the Lord came down, caused an earthquake, rolled away the stone, and sat on top of it. "His countenance was like lightning, and his clothing as white as snow" (Matthew 28:2–3). The guards "fell down as dead men."

Just as angels announced Jesus' birth to the shepherds, now an angel "announces" his resurrection to the Roman guards. As so often in Scripture, the message of God's love and grace is delivered to people the world would consider unworthy.

The angel encouraged the women who had arrived and announced the wondrous resurrection of Jesus. He instructed them to tell the other disciples. They ran to do so. The guards, however, ran to tell the chief priests. The priests bribed them to spread the rumor that the disciples stole the body.

There was no angelic announcement, and no divine fireworks. An event as spectacular as a resurrection would seem to warrant an exclamation so grand it would be overwhelming. Instead, we have the opposite, with word spreading slowly, person to person. People simply believing, half-believing, or disbelieving, spreading the news that Jesus was alive.

Perhaps this says that God loves faith—though God is perfectly capable of overwhelming the senses, he chooses not to. He presents the truth in human-size nuggets and invites us to believe.

Thomas was the most reluctant of Jesus' disciples to believe. No matter how many friends told him they had seen Jesus, he refused to believe. He said, "Unless I see in His hands the print of the nails, and put my finger into the print of the nails, and put my hand into His side, I will not believe" (John 20:25).

Jesus later engages Thomas in a dramatic scene. He invites his friend to touch the nail prints in his hands and the scar in his side from the sword. Thomas falls to his knees to confess Jesus as "My Lord and My God" (John 20:28).

Jesus calls him blessed for seeing and believing and declares a blessing on those who "have not seen and yet believed" (John 20:29). ◆

## { COUNTING THE DAYS }

How long was Jesus in the grave? If Jesus was crucified on a Friday and raised again on a Sunday, how could he claim he would be in the grave for "three days and three nights in the heart of the Earth" (Matthew 12:40)? The simple answer lies in the Jewish manner of speech for reckoning days. For example, Esther calls for fasting "for three days, night or day," which is later spoken of as "on the third day" (4:16, 5:1). The phrases "on the third day" and "three days and three nights" were equivalent. Jesus died on Friday and rose again, as promised, on the third day.

The Cross on Mount Strymba
overlooks the village of Kolochava,
Ukraine, in the Carpathian Mountains.

# 7

## The Cosmic Christ

# THE
# UNSEEN JESUS

THE MOST UNKNOWN CHRIST IS THE MISUNDERSTOOD ONE. HE IS
NO LONGER THE MAN WE THINK WE KNOW AND VARIOUSLY VISUALIZE.
HE'S NOT WEARING A WHITE ROBE AND SITTING ON A PARK BENCH
IN HEAVEN WAITING FOR US TO JOIN HIM. HE'S EVERYWHERE
AND IN EVERYTHING. AND, IN FACT, HE ALWAYS WAS.

CHRIST IS NOT JESUS' LAST NAME. THIS STATEMENT might appear flippant, puzzling and perhaps annoying. We have so associated Jesus and Christ that the two words are glued together and even considered synonymous, which they most certainly are not.

We are startled when we see the two separated in the Bible, as in: "Know for certain that God has made him both Lord and Christ, this Jesus whom you crucified" (Acts 2:36); or "[Simeon] had been told by the Holy Spirit he would not see death until he had seen the Christ of God" (Luke 2:26).

In other words, Jesus and Christ do not signify the same thing.

So, if Jesus of Nazareth was conceived in Mary and given his name, which we understand to mean "God Saves," what is Christ? That comes from the Greek, and means "The Anointed One," corresponding to the Hebrew word for "Messiah." But who is anointed, who anoints, and what is the anointing? The Human/Created is anointed by the Divine/Uncreated, with the anointing of the Holy Spirit, and the result is a marriage of the Human and Divine, Created and Uncreated, sealed with the Spirit of Love.

Or, if you will, Christ is God as manifest in the world, and manifest in humanity as Jesus.

Of course, the Christ mystery is manifest in the cosmos long before the birth of Jesus of Nazareth. So, Christ is cosmic from the start. If one states this, one is immediately accused of being "New Age," whereas it is loudly and gloriously proclaimed in the New Testament. But no one ever preaches on or discusses these passages, since they are scary and not understood, and way too magnificent and challenging to be let into our comfortable and circumscribed lives.

When was the last time you heard a pastor in a megachurch, or even a Catholic priest, preach on Colossians 1:

*He is the Image of the Invisible God, the Firstborn of All Creation, since in Him all things were created, in heaven or upon the Earth, whether visible or invisible…all things were created through him and for him. He is before all things, and in him all things hold together.*

As the Franciscan friar and spiritual writer Richard Rohr points out in his remarkable and landmark book, *The Universal Christ*, this message seems to be foundational, since it constitutes the first chapter of so many New Testament writings: John 1,

The dome of St. Peter's Basilica dominates Vatican City, the world's smallest country, nestled in the heart of Rome.

This image of Christ's Sacred Heart, exposed and wrapped in thorns, is on display in Slovakia.

1 John 1, Hebrews 1, Colossians 1, Ephesians 1. Yet we still have missed and ignored it.

But if our Christ is way too small and parochial, part of the problem is that our God is way too small as well! If the prologue of John's Gospel proclaims: "In the beginning was the Word, and the Word was with God, and the Word was God," then who is this God of whom we speak? If we imagine (and it is an imagining!) a bearded old white man on a throne, our God is not only too tiny and inadequate, but a blasphemous idol! Because God is infinite, or—to put it differently—God is not a Being, but Being itself, as St. Augustine and St. Thomas Aquinas assert.

Despite what the Catechism says, God is not the Supreme Being, as if just the highest in a hierarchy of the category of Beings. God is Uncreated, Infinite Being. His Son/Word is likewise infinite, as is the dynamic spirit of love between them.

From this divine dance, the universe is spun out with unimaginable energy and joy, and God is manifest in Christ, as St. Paul triumphantly announces in the Epistle to the Colossians. Or as he points out in Hebrews 1:2–3:

> God has spoken to us in his Son, whom he has appointed the heir of all things, and through whom he created the universe. He is the reflection of His glory, and bears the stamp of his nature, sustaining all things by the Word of His Power.

In modern terms, we might say that the mystery of Christ is present from the moment of the Big Bang, the first revelation or manifestation of God, dynamically present in and to his creation as the source of being and energy.

IT IS NO SURPRISE THAT ONE OF THE CONSEQUENCES of envisioning God as the Supreme Being, separate and sitting on a throne wielding power, is that we see Christ in the same way: a separate individual, Jesus, sitting at God's right hand, with immense power and dignity, indeed divine dignity, but basically reduced to a separate, identifiable man. Just as it is formally correct but highly misleading to call

the Bible the "Word of God," so it is formally correct but highly misleading to call Jesus "God." Both are a commingling of human and divine, the Word of God in the obscure and imperfect words of men (Scripture), and the Word of God in the humanity of Jesus of Nazareth. The only reason we can even refer to Jesus as God is by favor of the medieval notion, never spoken about, called the *communicatio idiomatum*, or "sharing of attributes" between the human and divine in Jesus. What this means: Because there is only One Divine Person in Jesus, but two natures—human and divine—what is said of one nature can be ascribed to the other by reason of the unity of person.

For example: We say, "God died on the cross," because the person, Jesus, died on the cross in his

> ## "AND THE WORD BECAME FLESH, AND DWELT AMONG US, AND WE SAW HIS GLORY."
> —*John 1:14*

human nature, rather than in the immortal divine nature. Similarly, "this Man is God" because we are speaking about the person, though really only his divine nature is divine. Early Christian history was driven, if not tortured, by this paradox and yo-yo back and forth. The Council of Ephesus in 431 defined Mary as the Mother of God, because a mother gives birth to a person, not just a nature, and here the person is divine.

Jesus' human nature was created and finite, joined to the divine in what theology calls the Hypostatic Union, but not divine: unfathomably close to God and unfathomably distant from God. What this means is that a cult of Jesus, reducing him just to the dimensions of our own limited humanity, even in his resurrection, is enormously dangerous and counterproductive. In this approach, the infinite dimensions of Christ's divinity are effectively ignored, denied and pushed aside. And if one counters with, "All of this is very abstract and abstruse, and not something we should have to bother ourselves with," I respectfully but insistently reply: "If the first several centuries of our Christian forebearers bothered themselves so energetically and laboriously over so many decades to get it right, surely we can spend a few hours making a small effort to understand it as well!" Why would we expect something so momentous to be easy?

The neglected cosmic dimension can be studied separately under the rubric "Christ." As Rohr

## "IT IS NO LONGER I WHO LIVE, BUT CHRIST WHO LIVES IN ME."
—*Galatians 2:20*

expresses it: "Christ is God, and Jesus is the Christ's historical manifestation in time. Jesus is a Third Someone, not just God, and not just human, but God and human together."

Yet, if these consequences of recognizing the cosmic Christ are so earthshaking and far-reaching for the creation of the universe, Christ as the Alpha (as in the Book of Revelation, 1), its ramifications and consequences for us are even more enthralling and shocking as we discover the untold and astounding dimensions of Christ the Omega.

Jesuit priest Pierre Teilhard de Chardin, in the first half of the 20th century, had a powerful, spiritually dynamic appreciation of the presence of God, and of Christ, in the material universe, unfolding and evolving with all the splendor and fervor of the spirit, toward the Omega Point, or its final fulfillment in Christ. For Teilhard's Catholic soul, this was implemented and symbolized by the Sacred Heart of Jesus, his humanity pulsating and exploding with love, and bestowing the Pentecostal Spirit.

This produced the richness and diversity of creation and humanity, and unified all dimensions together in what Teilhard called a Phylum of Love, the love he rightly saw as the fundamental energy of the cosmos, leading to its consummation in God. Many theologians and writers enthusiastically corroborate his vision, such as Ilia Delio and Beatrice Bruteau. The famous Catalan theologian Raimon Panikkar coined a neologism for this cosmic reality, following Teilhard who also loved neologisms: "Cosmotheandric." This is a combination of three Greek words: *cosmos* (world), *theos* (God), and *andros* (man). In the final synthesis, God, world and humanity are one intimately integrated and interrelated reality.

Lest we think this is just the product of a fervid and overexcited imagination, let us return to Scripture, to the sources of this constantly neglected vision of the cosmic Christ, precisely as it plays out in his Paschal mystery, his cross and resurrection, his passage toward becoming Omega.

As the Jesuit theologian Ladislaus Boros put it:
When Christ's human reality was planted in death right at the heart of the world, within the deepest stratum of the universe, the stratum that unites at root bottom all that the world is, at that moment in his bodily humanity he became the real ontological ground of a new universal scheme of salvation embracing the whole human race.

Here is where the cosmic Christ reveals its fullest and most challenging dimensions: Jesus' resurrection was not the resuscitation of a corpse, the resumption of his ordinary, earthbound human life, but an explosion of light and the expansion of his entire humanity, body, heart and soul, into the very dimensions of the universe. He is now, as Paul boldly puts it in Colossians 1:18, "the firstborn of the dead"—more than that, Christ is now the "head of the Body of the Church, the fullness of Him who fills the universe in all its parts," Paul explains in Ephesians 1:22–23, The text literally says "fills all in all." No wonder he could pass through walls, appear and disappear, and go unrecognized, no longer limited to his previous life and appearance!

*Creation of Adam*
By Michelangelo
1512, painted on the ceiling of
the Sistine Chapel, Vatican City

How do many of us encounter Christ in the hidden depths of our hearts, instead of praying to him as some circumscribed objective reality external to ourselves? "So that rooted and grounded in love, you may comprehend with all the Saints what is the length and breadth and height and depth"— how cosmic!—"and know the Love of Christ, which surpasses knowledge, and be filled with the very fullness of God" (Ephesians 3:17–19).

These four amazing traits are later named by St. Thomas Aquinas: impassibility (cannot suffer or die); clarity (blazing with light and glory); agility (the ability to pass from one end of the universe to the other without time or distance); and subtlety (spiritualization—we would say energy today, both particle and wave). Pure energy and light, taking any form it wishes! That is hardly the image we have of the afterlife, getting our bodies back and standing around a heavenly court, waving palm branches!

Finally, in fact, there will only be Christ, as so many mystics triumphantly acclaim. St. Augustine famously and mysteriously said: "In the end, there will just be One Christ, loving Himself." As Christ ascended into the bosom of the father, the bottomless abyss of God, so will we be absorbed in God with him. The eternal Christ alone will remain of the created world: "It is no longer I who live, but Christ who lives in Me" (Galatians 2:20).

How could Christ be Omega, if there were anything other than he? —*Father Michael K. Holleran*

Hinduism regards
Christ as a prophet;
some sects regard him as
a Shaktavesha Avatar,
an incarnation of
God on Earth.

Mosaic artwork from
Thailand, displayed
at the Church of the
Annunciation in
Nazareth, Israel.

# JESUS IN
# OTHER RELIGIONS

ALL MAJOR FAITHS ACKNOWLEDGE JESUS,
BUT DO THEY BELIEVE HE IS THE SON OF GOD?

### JUDAISM

Orthodox Jews look upon Jesus as a false prophet, not the long-awaited (and still-expected) Messiah. Further, as confirmed monotheists whose central principle is, "Our God is One," they consider the worship of any man a form of idolatry. Most Jewish views of Jesus have traditionally been negative. But the Spanish Jewish physician/poet Judah Halevi (1075–1141) and the Sephardic philosopher Moses Maimonides (1138–1204) both viewed Jesus as an important preparatory figure for the coming Messianic Age. Other than his followers, most Jews refused to believe that Jesus was the Messiah, believing he never fulfilled the prophecies, nor had the necessary qualifications of one.

### ISLAM

Muslims revere all prophets from the Torah, the Bible and the Quran. Devout Muslims recognize Jews and Christians as fellow "people of the Book," because all three religions originated with Abraham, and all have divine revelations enshrined in books. Islam respects Jesus, whom they call "Isa," and it's the only faith besides Christianity that accepts the miraculous birth of Jesus from a virgin mother. Indeed, Mary is treated with the highest honor and respect in the Quran. Muslims do not consider Jesus the Son of God, but a "divine messenger," who received inspiration directly from God. Islam holds that the original message was somehow distorted or lost, and therefore the New Testament is not an accurate account of Allah's message to humanity.

### HINDUISM

Hinduism is an ancient and diverse collection of religious/philosophical beliefs. The faith's principal holy book, the Bhagavad Gita, originated almost 5,000 years ago, long before Christianity or Islam existed. In Hindu theology, God belongs to no one religion. Rather, all religions are paths that lead to him. Nonetheless, some gurus consider Jesus a Shaktavesha Avatar, a human incarnation of a deity, perhaps of Krishna.

### BUDDHISM

Buddhists call Jesus "Isha"; he is well-respected as a prophet in the tradition of Gautama (also called Siddhartha). Little is studied of the life of Jesus among Buddhists, whose focus is on transcendental concepts, rather than being personality oriented.

### SIKHISM

Sikhism (from the Punjabi word for "seeker" or "aspirant") is a monotheistic religion that originated in the northwestern Indian state of Punjab. Dating from the 15th century, it is one of the youngest major faiths, and the world's fifth largest organized religion. Although Jesus is seen by Sikhs as a holy man and saint, they do not believe in his divinity, since their faith holds that God is never born, and never dies. ◆

# FALSE PROPHETS

IN JESUS' TIME, OTHER MEN CLAIMED TO BE THE MESSIAH.
THEY USUALLY HAD A MORE EARTHLY PRIORITY, HOWEVER:
FREEING THE JEWS FROM OPPRESSION.

THOSE WHO DON'T BELIEVE IN GOD AND IN THE miraculous life of Christ like to point out that there was nothing particularly special about Jesus, and that there were many others who proclaimed themselves leader of the Jews and the promised Messiah, and who were crucified, or otherwise dispatched.

## "THERE WERE QUITE A FEW FIGURES WHO WERE MESSIAHS OR HEALERS OR PROPHETS."
—*Helen K. Bond, PhD*

Some critics of Christianity have posited that Jesus, if he even existed at all, was simply following in, or created whole-cloth from, the tradition of a multitude of Messianic figures, some from a century before his birth.

But cold historical fact, and an understanding of the strict mandates of the Jewish religion, undermine that claim. First of all, there is little record of many figures developing followers and attempting to lead the Jews, and none of them proclaimed themselves to be the Son of God. And under Jewish guidelines, a Messiah had to, among other things, be a perfect teacher of God's commandments, rebuild the temple in Jerusalem, and be a male from the House of David—a not surprisingly high disqualifier.

At the time that Jesus was born, Judea had been part of the Roman Empire since 63 B.C., the year of Pompey's Siege of Jerusalem. This was a time of great social unrest, with the Judean population regularly rising up against the Romans. The region of Judea "was known for being a hotbed of political activity, some of it violent.... In historical context, that region was always a contested region," said Allen D. Callahan, PhD, of Harvard Divinity School, during a PBS interview in 1998.

A number of alleged prophets appeared during this era, some claiming to be the long-awaited Messiah. Most were snared and brutally punished by the Romans. Jesus was not the only upstart who was publicly crucified: That was the common penalty the Romans meted out to discourage dissidents.

The first-century Jewish historian Flavius Josephus shows "that there were a bunch of fanatics in Palestine who were running around causing trouble, whipping up the local yokels. And that these people were irresponsible and they weren't representative. And that the Romans could deal with them and dispatch them quickly. Josephus' point is that they are fanatics; they're not responsible people," explains Callahan.

*St. John the Baptist Preaching*
By Mattia Preti
1665

In reality, St. John the Baptist would have been skinnier than in this 17th-century painting, since he reportedly lived on honey and insects.

*St. John baptized Jesus in the River Jordan, but proclaimed that Jesus "shall baptize you in the Holy Spirit and in fire."*
—Matthew 3:11

*The Baptism of Christ*
By Christoph Schwarz
ca. 1575–80

Here are some men, other than Jesus, who were also considered potential Messiahs:

## THE ESSENES PREACHER

About 100 B.C., this firebrand (his actual name is unknown) formed a sect known as the Essenes. He gathered several hundred followers to live in the desert (near where the Dead Sea Scrolls were found), where they waited for the Messiah.

### "BEHOLD THE LAMB OF GOD, WHO TAKES AWAY THE SIN OF THE WORLD."
*—John 1:29*

The Essenes believed it was their mission to fight the Sons of Darkness, who would presumably appear near the end of the world. Many Essenes lived in caves and practiced baptism. Some scholars believe they influenced Jesus' teachings. They preached salvation, but selective salvation, not for all people. The Romans, who were on their naughty list, eliminated the Essenes in A.D. 68.

## JOHN THE BAPTIST

Later came this wandering, eccentric Jewish preacher (in the late decades B.C. to approximately A.D. 28–36) who baptized Jesus and who spurned the mantle of Messiah by telling his ardent followers, "One who will baptize with the Holy Spirit" was coming, and that he, John, was just preparing the way for Jesus.

John the Baptist is known as an ascetic who wore a loincloth and subsisted on a diet of locusts and honey. Some claim that John was an Essene, and that Jesus probably inherited some of his earliest followers from John's flock.

New Testament sources state that John was condemned to death by Herod Antipas after rebuking him for divorcing his wife in order to marry his brother's wife. John was famously beheaded upon the request of Salome (she is thought to have been influenced by her mother).

### SIMON OF PERAEA

Although some debate whether he actually claimed to be a Messiah, Simon of Peraea, a former slave of Herod the Great (father of Herod Antipas), tried to foment a rebellion. It was suppressed and he was executed by Roman centurions between 4 B.C. and A.D. 14.

### ATHRONGES

After King Herod the Great died in 4 B.C., this tall, burly shepherd attempted to usurp the Judean throne. He and several of his brothers started a guerrilla war against Rome, but ultimately failed.

## "JESUS ASKED THEM, 'BUT WHO DO YOU SAY THAT I AM?' PETER ANSWERED HIM, 'YOU ARE THE CHRIST.'"

—Mark 8:29

### THEUDAS

As the historian Josephus reported, around the year A.D. 44, Theudas claimed to be a prophet of the Lord and attracted a following of many hundreds of people. He commanded them to bring their belongings and come with him to the River Jordan, where he announced that, as proof of his holiness, he would divide the waters as Moses once had. But the Roman procurator Cuspius Fadus sent a cavalry troop to intercept them before they could reach their destination. The Romans killed many of Theudas' disciples, and then brought Theudas' severed head back with them to Fadus.

### JUDAS THE GALILEAN

No, it's not that Judas. This one was a troublemaker for the Romans, with no claim to divinity, who led a resistance movement against Roman taxation around A.D. 6. He urged Jews not to register, and

his followers punished those who insisted on following the tax law by burning their houses and stealing their cattle.

Judas the Galilean himself was eventually captured and executed, but his family continued the rebellion in his stead. Subsequently, two of his sons were crucified by the Roman governor sometime around A.D. 40.

At that time, "Galilee may have become a center of, not only social dissent, but economic protest. There seems to be a rise of what we might describe as social banditry," says L. Michael White, PhD, director of the Institute for the Study of Antiquity and Christian Origins at the University of Texas at Austin.

### THE EGYPTIAN

This was another colorful character whose name is now lost in history. In his day, he laid claim to a variety of magical powers. In doing so, he apparently attracted a great many followers—some estimate as many as 30,000 people—and led them in a revolt against the Romans around the middle of the first century. But unlike most other rabble-rousers, who ended up being crucified or otherwise slaughtered, the Egyptian was able to make a clean getaway before being captured by the Romans. Unfortunately, many of his followers were not so lucky.

As Josephus wrote, somewhat dismissively, in his text *The Jewish War*:

> "There was an Egyptian false prophet that did the Jews more mischief than the former; for he was a cheat, and pretended to be a prophet also, and got together 30,000 men that were deluded by him; these he led round about from the wilderness to the mount which was called the Mount of Olives. He was ready to break into Jerusalem by force from that place; and if he could but once conquer the Roman garrison and the people, he intended to rule them by the assistance of those guards of his that were to break into the city with him." ◆

*Salome With the Head
of St. John the Baptist*
By Lucas Caranach, the Elder
ca. 1510

For his
unwavering faith
and advocacy that
Christ was the
savior, St. John
the Baptist was
beheaded.

Saint Augustine
By Philippe de Champaigne
1650

St. Augustine wrote: "Seek not to understand that you may believe, but believe that you may understand."

# JESUS WAS
## MALE, RIGHT?

HE LIVED AND DIED AS A MAN, BUT OTHERS ARGUE
HE ACTUALLY TRANSCENDS GENDER.

AT THE RISK OF BEING INFURIATING, IT MUST BE stated that this Christ is beyond gender. Jesus, of course, is male, but Christ is before and beyond male, the perfect, primordial blend of masculine and feminine, just as God is!

To be sure, Jesus calls God his father for who knows how many valid reasons (theological, psychological, social), and so will Christians always likewise. But the divinity completely transcends gender, formally and eminently, containing all the perfection of both masculine and feminine.

> ### "ALLOW YOUR HEART TO OPEN TOWARD THAT INVISIBLE BUT ALWAYS PRESENT ORIGIN OF ALL THAT EXISTS."
> —Cynthia Bourgeault

The theologian Sister Elizabeth Johnson, PhD, wrote a book about the Divine Being and identity called *She Who Is*. And one of the richest conceptual formulations of this idea, clearly reflective of deep devotion and conducive to it, is the phrase popularized by Cynthia Bourgeault, PhD, a contemporary writer and mystic: "ChristoSophia". *Sophia*, "wisdom" in Greek, is feminine (as it is in Hebrew and Latin).

The Book of Proverbs, therefore, in the famous cosmic chapter 8, speaks of wisdom as "she," present with God in the beginning as his architect and firstborn, delighting in creation and in the "children of men." Christian commentators long tended to ascribe this figure to Mary, the Mother of Jesus. Yet Christ is deemed the Wisdom and Power of God (1 Corinthians 1) and the Firstborn of all Creation (Colossians 1), and thus includes all feminine characteristics as well.

As Bourgeault remarks, this primordial figure, ChristoSophia, is at the "headwaters of gender," and reminds us that the masculine, much less the male, in no way has primacy over the feminine.

In the book *Mary Magdalene: The Christos-Sophia Revelation*, Jewels Maloney writes: "The voice of The Magdalene [was] heard in story, film, sacred texts, oral traditions that were finally being written down and disseminated, and from people connecting with The Magdalene energies and channeling her messages of love, truth and wisdom. Many...have felt the call of The Magdalene in their hearts, and have joined in this great journey of... demonstrating the Feminine and the Masculine Christ Consciousness, which brings into fruition a new wholeness, unity, unconditional love and creative joy."

And as the 14th-century mystic Julian of Norwich sweetly, startlingly asserted, "Jesus is our Mother"!
—*Father Michael K. Holleran*

Was the Holy Grail a dish, a chalice—or something else? For centuries, we've wondered.

*The Last Supper*
By Leandro Dal Ponte Bassano
1542

# THE
## HOLY GRAIL

EVERYONE IS FAMILIAR WITH THE LEGEND,
BUT DID IT EVER ACTUALLY EXIST?

JUST BEFORE THE BEGINNING OF THE 13TH CENTURY, between 1181 and 1190, French poet Chrétien de Troyes wrote *Perceval, the Story of the Grail*. This is credited as the first literary account of the Holy Grail, the cup held by Christ, but his story doesn't fully resemble the one we've come to know.

Chrétien's *graal* is a plate, not a cup or goblet. John Carey, PhD, professor of Early and Medieval Irish studies at the University College Cork, says, "Here the Grail is a splendid golden dish, shining with supernatural light, which appears in a mysterious castle to the young knight Perceval [one of King Arthur's knights].

"Much later in the story," Carey continues, "Perceval is told by a hermit that the Grail is 'very holy,' and that it contains a Eucharistic wafer, but that is all. It is not said to be linked with Christ, or Christ's Passion."

Invited to spend the night as a guest of a curious king, Perceval sees the dish in passing and later comes to understand that the plate has healing properties. Chrétien never completed his story, but four different writers continued it after his death.

It's likely that elements of Chrétien's story already existed as oral tales and minstrel songs across Europe. "Medieval authors don't usually create a whole plot, they usually are continuing a tradition," says Christopher Snyder, PhD, professor of history and dean at Mississippi State University. "One theory is that there were bards who traveled [from] court to court singing songs and it was part of medieval culture for centuries."

In the early 13th century, another French poet, Robert de Boron, brought the Holy Grail to a new level. "It is de Boron who changed the Grail from a dish (which is what *graal* means in Old French) to a chalice; and it is he who said that it was the cup from which Christ drank at the Last Supper, and in which Joseph of Arimathea [who provided Christ's

> ## "*THIS CUP IS THE NEW COVENANT IN MY BLOOD, WHICH IS POURED OUT FOR YOU.*"
> —*Luke 22:20*

tomb and took his body down from the Cross] subsequently gathered Christ's blood when he was being taken from the Cross," says Carey.

"The Grail legend is most likely a combination of pagan magic wonder tales and what we would call 'Christian mythology,' which is sort of the stories that involve biblical figures that circulated, some of them very early on, even in the second century A.D., but were not canonized," says Snyder.

Other authors, including an anonymous French writer who wrote *The Quest for the Holy Grail*, added layers to the folklore of Arthur, but the cornerstone of the mythology is *Le Morte d'Arthur,* written by English poet and knight Sir Thomas Malory and first published in 1485, who reconstituted the general narrative (which by now included a wizard, Merlin) and added new material. Whereas originally Perceval had stumbled across the Grail, now King Arthur's Knights of the Round Table were dispatched across the known world to find it.

We also have the interrelated story of the Knights Templar. (Their official name is Poor Fellow-Soldiers of Christ and of the Temple of Solomon, so you can see why they settled on Knights Templar.) Founded

## *"I BELIEVE WHOEVER SEES THE GRAIL WILL FIND IT AGREEABLE..."*
—*Robert de Boron, 13th century French poet*

in 1119 as a Catholic order by French knight Hugues de Payens, they were blessed by the pope and exempted by him from all laws, so were a particularly ruthless spearhead of the crusades in the first half of the 12th century. Legend has it they discovered the Holy Grail in Jerusalem, and brought it back to England with them, and according to some versions of the legend, it's still there.

AS FAR AS ANYONE CAN TELL, NONE OF THIS IS TRUE. The Knights Templar flourished until the 1300s, when prevailing French and papal politics destroyed their order and most of the Knights were executed, but they never had the Grail. Neither they nor anyone else looked for it, and it never turned up in England.

And that's to say nothing of the vast unlikelihood that an ordinary cup would have survived from Christ's Last Supper until nearly 1,000 years later. "There is no historical evidence that there was any specific quest or a war fought for or over the Grail," says Snyder.

"Arthur himself as a major figure of the Dark Ages was a late construct, originating in the ninth

century in a Welsh Latin text, the *Historia Brittonum,* dreamed up by an author keen to place British figures who were both Christian and successful in battle in front of his audience at a time of great danger to the Welsh people," says Nicholas J. Higham, PhD, a professor emeritus of history at the University of Manchester and the co-author of *The Anglo-Saxon World.*

"We can say that the Grail, wherever it came from, does not seem to have been associated with the story of Christ's passion originally," says Carey. "The idea of Arthur's knights collectively embarking in search of the Grail arose later still."

According to Higham: "Many people still think Arthur has some sort of historical reality. The fact remains, though, that he does not occur in any historical literature before the ninth century work that has [any] historical reliability whatsoever."

The great irony is that there is one group who apparently did look for the Grail, delusionally believing it to have magical powers—the Nazis! During World War II, Heinrich Himmler, the head of the SS, backed an expedition led by Otto Rahn, an eccentric historian obsessed with the legend of Arthur. Rahn believed the Grail was last in the possession of the Cathars, a medieval religious sect in Southern Europe who were deemed heretics and wiped out in the 13th century. He led a search across Northern Italy and Southern France, but failed to find anything and wound up banished to a concentration camp as a guard and ultimately took his own life.

The overwhelming lack of evidence doesn't stop people from claiming they actually have the Grail. According to a 2019 article in *History,* there are about 200 vessels around the world, in monasteries, churches and castles, that backers claim are the actual chalice with which Christ performed the first transubstantiation, the first Holy Communion. Many have been seriously (and inconclusively!) investigated, including by the Vatican.

Because it's a physical link to Jesus' last night on Earth as a human, the Holy Grail remains one of history and Catholicism's most enduring and endearing legends. But, alas, it is just a myth. ◆

Galahad on the Seat Perilous,
the Holy Grail Appears
By Évrard d'Espinques
1470

Did the Knights
of the Round Table
actually seek the
Holy Grail?
Probably not.

## ZION

First mentioned in 2 Samuel 5:7, and cited 152 times in the Hebrew Bible, Zion was used in the Old Testament to refer to Mount Zion—a hill found in Jerusalem. It would eventually become a synonym for Jerusalem and then the entire biblical land of Israel.

# IN THE
## FOOTSTEPS
## OF JESUS

COME ALONG ON A JOURNEY TO THE
LANDS OF THE BIBLE FOR THE CHANCE
TO SEE WHERE JESUS WALKED
AND LIVED MILLENNIA AGO.

THE NAMES OF THE PLACES ARE ALL FAMILIAR TO us, of course: Jerusalem, Nazareth, Bethlehem, Mount Zion. Some are now bustling, modern cities, with their ancient sites still intact as a part of daily life for residents. Others are smaller, with recent excavations uncovering more evidence of what life was like for those who lived in Bible times. Today, nearly all remain sacred places for Christians, Jews and Muslims.

What compels millions of people of all faiths to visit these sites every year? For many, it's the opportunity of a lifetime to feel a deeper connection to their history and gain more understanding of their religious faith. Many wish to learn what Jesus' daily life must have felt like, and to see what he saw so long ago. Although the Bible tells us the names of these places, many of us feel compelled to experience them for ourselves.

These photos will show you what these ancient locations look like today as you learn more about their importance to the Bible-dwellers who lived and worked there alongside Jesus. Perhaps you'll feel inspired to make your own pilgrimage to the spots so familiar to us through their vivid descriptions in the Bible. ◆

### JESUS TRAIL
This 40-mile route in Galilee is popular for hikers and pilgrims alike, as walkers can connect each step with the life of Christ. The trail begins in Nazareth and passes through well-known towns like Capernaum and Sepphoris.

### NAZARETH
The town of Nazareth, in Galilee, is where Gabriel told Mary she'd give birth to Jesus, and it's where he spent the first 31 years of his life. Nazareth is first mentioned in the Bible in the Gospels.

**BETHLEHEM**
It's in Micah 5:2 that Bethlehem, a village 5 miles south of Jerusalem, is established as the birthplace of the future king—a prophecy fulfilled by Jesus' birth.

**AL-MAGHTAS**
Pilgrims can not only visit but also be baptized in the same place where John baptized Jesus Christ. In fact, over half a million tourists do so each year. The site offers 12 separate baptismal pools for groups to worship privately.

**MOUNT PRECIPICE**
When the angry Nazarene mob drove Jesus to the cliff, it was at the top of Mount Precipice, located just south of Jesus' hometown, in the cliffs of Mount Kedumim.

**TABGHA**
Traditionally considered to be the place of Jesus' miracle of bread and fish multiplication, Tabgha is also the spot of his fourth known appearance after his resurrection.

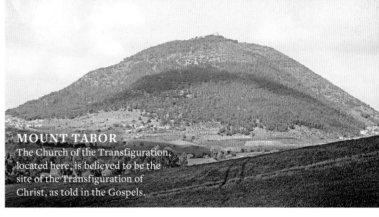

**MOUNT TABOR**
The Church of the Transfiguration, located here, is believed to be the site of the Transfiguration of Christ, as told in the Gospels.

**SIDON**
"From there [Jesus] arose and went away to the region of Tyre and Sidon"(Mark 7:24). Jesus visited the wealthy port of Sidon, a Phoenician city about 25 miles from Tyre.

**SEA OF GALILEE**
Here, Jesus performed one of his most famous miracles when he walked across the water to board a storm-tossed ship full of his disciples, calmed the seas and helped them sail to safety.

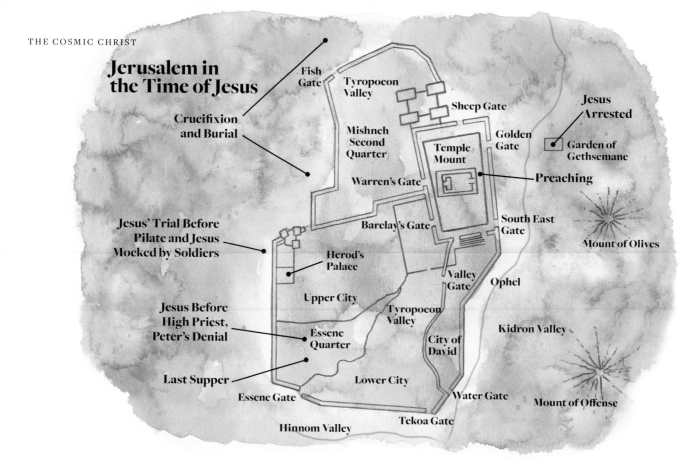

## Jerusalem in the Time of Jesus

Fish Gate

Tyropoeon Valley

Sheep Gate

**Crucifixion and Burial**

Mishneh (Second Quarter)

Golden Gate

**Jesus Arrested**

Temple Mount

Garden of Gethsemane

Warren's Gate

**Preaching**

Jesus' Trial Before Pilate and Jesus Mocked by Soldiers

Barclay's Gate

South East Gate

Mount of Olives

Herod's Palace

Valley Gate

Ophel

Upper City

Jesus Before High Priest, Peter's Denial

Tyropoeon Valley

City of David

Kidron Valley

Essene Quarter

Last Supper

Lower City

Water Gate

Mount of Offense

Essene Gate

Tekoa Gate

Hinnom Valley

### THE LAST SUPPER
Depicted in one of the world's most famous paintings, The Last Supper is thought to have taken place outside the walls of the Old City of Jerusalem, on Mount Zion.

### CALVARY
Since the fourth century, this has been considered the site of Jesus' crucifixion, where the Church of the Holy Sepulchre stands today. In the Bible, it's said to be near Jerusalem.

## JERUSALEM

Located between the Mediterranean Sea and the Dead Sea, this city was the site of many of Jesus' visits and miracles, and ultimately, his death.

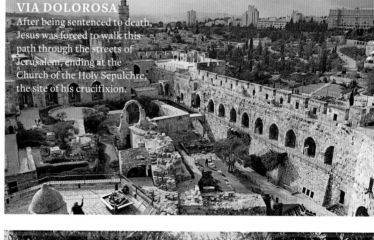

## VIA DOLOROSA

After being sentenced to death, Jesus was forced to walk this path through the streets of Jerusalem, ending at the Church of the Holy Sepulchre, the site of his crucifixion.

## POOL OF BETHESDA

The Pool of Bethesda (now a ruin) is best remembered as the place where Jesus healed a paralyzed man.

## MOUNT OF OLIVES

As told in the Acts of the Apostles, this is the spot, east of Jerusalem's Old City, where Jesus ascended to heaven. The mountain has been a Jewish cemetery for over 3,000 years.

## CREDITS

**COVER** Popperfoto/Getty **FRONT FLAP** Carl Simon/United Archives/Universal Images Group/Getty; Andrey Kuzmin/ Shutterstock **2-3** Peter Horree/Alamy **4-5** GoneWithTheWind/Shutterstock **6-7** Fred de Noyelle/Getty **8-9** Anton Petrus/Getty **10-11** Sasha Taran/Shutterstock **12-13** *From left:* Asar Studios/Alamy; Miguel Nicolaevsky/500px/Getty **14-15** Godong/Universal Images Group/Getty **16-17** *From left:* Fine Art Images/Heritage Images/Getty; Prisma Archivo/ Alamy **18-19** *From left:* Manuel Cohen/Aurimages/Zuma; DeAgostini/Getty **20-21** *From left:* Fotosearch/Getty; Historic Images/Alamy **22-23** Fine Art Images/Heritage Images/Getty **24-25** *From left:* Arte & Immagini srl/Corbis/Getty; Art Media/Print Collector/Getty **26-27** *From left:* Dea/G. Cigolini/De Agostini/Getty; DeAgostini/Getty **28-29** Fine Art Images/Heritage Images/Getty **30-31** Godong/Universal Images Group/Getty **32-33** Duckycards/Getty **34-35** *From left:* Bridgeman Art Library/Getty; DeAgostini/A. Dagli Orti/Getty **36-37** DeAgostini/G. Dagli Orti/Getty **38-39** *From left:* Duncan1890/Getty, Steve Stankiewicz **40-41** *From left:* Culture Club/Getty; Richard T. Nowitz/Getty **42-43** VCG Wilson/ Corbis/Getty; Fotografica Foglia/Electa/Mondadori Portfolio/Getty **44-45** Album/Alamy **46-47** *From left:* Jozef Sedmak/ Alamy; Denis Waugh/Getty **48-49** *From left:* DeAgostini/A Dagli Orti/Getty; Christine Osborne/World Religions Photo Library/Alamy **50-51** *From left:* J. Lopez Photography/Shutterstock, Steve Stankiewicz **52-53** *From left:* Print Collector/ Getty; DeAgostini/Archivio J Lange/Getty **54-55** *From left:* Fine Art Images/Heritage Images/Getty; Peter Schickert/ Alamy **56-57** Photos.com/Getty **58-59** *From left:* Adolfo Bezzi/Electa/Mondadori Portfolio/Getty; De Agostini/A Dagli Orti/Getty **60-61** *From left:* Duncan1890/Getty, Steve Stankiewicz **62-63** *From left:* DeAgostini/G Dagli Orti/Getty; Luis Dafos/Getty **64-65** *From left:* DeAgostini/A De Gregorio/Getty; Peter Horree/Alamy **66-67** Album/Alamy **68-69** Picturenow/Universal Images Group/Getty **70-71** Giorgio Liverani/Electa /Mondadori Portfolio/Getty **72-73** Jozef Sedmak/Alamy **74-75** Sedmak/Getty **76-77** Sedmak/Getty **78-79** Fine Art Images/Heritage Image Partnership Ltd/Alamy **80-81** *From left:* Heritage Image Partnership Ltd/Fine Art Images/Alamy; Hindu Art/Alamy **82-83** Mint Images/Art Wolfe/Getty **84-85** Gianni Dagli Orti/Shutterstock **86-87** Print Collector/Getty **88-89** *From left:* David Lopez/EyeEm/ Getty; DeAgostini/G Dagli Orti/Getty **90-91** Godong/Alamy **92-93** DeAgostini/A De Gregorio/Getty **94-95** Adolfo Bezzi/Electa/Mondadori Portfolio/Getty **96-97** *From left:* Fine Art Images/Heritage Images/Getty; Mauritius Images GmbH/Alamy **98-99** Fine Art Images/Heritage Images/Getty **100-101** Peter Horree/Alamy **102-103** Fine Art Photographic Library/Corbis/Getty **104-105** Ann Ronan Pictures/Print Collector/Getty **106-107** *From left:* Fine Art Images/Heritage Images/Getty; DeAgostini/A Dagli Orti/Getty **108-109** Fine Art Images/Heritage Images/Getty **110-111** Time Life Pictures/Mansell/Life Picture Collection/Getty **112-113** Ann Ronan Pictures/Print Collector/Getty (2) **114-115** *Clockwise from bottom left:* Leemage/Corbis via Getty; Eric Vandeville/Gamma-Rapho/Getty; Culture Club/Getty **116-117** *From left:* Art Collection 2/Alamy; DeAgostini/Dea Picture Library/Getty **118-119** Alexey Fedoren/Getty **120-121** Album/ Alamy **122-123** Fine Art Images/Heritage Images/Getty **124-125** Album/Alamy **126-127** *From left:* Godong/Universal Images Group/Getty; World History Archive/Alamy **128-129** Blaine Harrington III/Alamy **130-131** Stockcreations/ Shutterstock **132-133** Peter Horree/Alamy **134-135** DeAgostini/Dea Picture Library/Getty **136-137** Fine Art Images/ Heritage Images/Getty **138-139** Art Collection 4/Alamy **140-141** Fine Art Images/Heritage Images/Getty **142-143** Imagno/ Getty **144-145** *From left:* Werner Forman/Universal Images Group/Getty; Godong/Universal Images Group/Getty **146-147** Heritage Art/Heritage Images/Getty **148-149** Carl Simon/United Archives/Universal Images Group/Getty **150-151** Art Collection 2/Alamy **152-153** *From left:* Art Media/Print Collector/Getty; Fine Art Images/Heritage Images/ Getty **154-155** Design Pics/Kristy-Anne Glubish/Getty; Godong/Universal Images Group/Getty **156-157** Fine Art Images/ Heritage Images/Getty **158-159** Panaramka/Getty **160-161** TTstudio/Getty **162-163** Sedmak/Getty **164-165** Creative Lab/ Shutterstock **166-167** Ryan Rodrick Beiler/Alamy **168-169** Mattia Preti/The AMICA Library/WikiPedia Commons **170-171** Prisma Archivo/Alamy **172-173** Incamerastock/Alamy **174-175** Courtesy Philippe de Champaigne/Los Angeles County Museum of Art/WikiPedia Commons **176-177** Vincenzo Fontana/Arte & Immagini srl/Corbis/Getty **178-179** Apic/ Getty **180-181** *Clockwise from left:* Chronicle/Alamy; Nir Alon/Alamy; Jason Langley/Alamy **182-183** *Clockwise from bottom left:* Vvvita/Alamy; Piero M. Bianchi/Getty; BonkersAboutTravel/Alamy; Itsik Marom/Alamy; Dbimages/Alamy; Shabtay/Shutterstock; John Theodor/Shutterstock **184-185** *Clockwise from bottom left:* ImageBroker/Alamy; Steve Stankiewicz; Gavin Hellier/Jon Arnold Images Ltd/Alamy; Richmatts/Getty; Tkachuk/Getty; Thierry64/Getty; Nikolay Vinokurov/Alamy **SPINE** Inked Pixels/Shutterstock **BACK FLAP** Jeff Vespa/WireImage/Getty; Andrey Kuzmin/Shutterstock **BACK COVER** DeAgostini/G. Dagli Orti/Getty; Fine Art Images/Heritage Images/Getty; Didecs/Shutterstock

### SPECIAL THANKS TO CONTRIBUTING WRITERS

Olivia Abel, Dean Christopher, Bill Giovannetti, Lukas Harnisch,
Father Michael K. Holleran, Jason Stahl

# CENTENNIAL BOOKS

An Imprint of
Centennial Media, LLC
40 Worth St., 10th Floor
New York, NY 10013, U.S.A.

CENTENNIAL BOOKS is a trademark of Centennial Media, LLC

ISBN 978-1-951274-55-9

Distributed by
Simon & Schuster, Inc.
1230 Avenue of the Americas
New York, NY 10020, U.S.A.

For information about custom editions, special sales and premium and corporate purchases, please contact Centennial Media at contact@centennialmedia.com.

Manufactured in Singapore

© 2021 by Centennial Media, LLC

10 9 8 7 6 5 4 3 2 1

**Publishers & Co-Founders** Ben Harris, Sebastian Raatz
**Editorial Director** Annabel Vered
**Creative Director** Jessica Power
**Executive Editor** Janet Giovanelli
**Deputy Editors** Ron Kelly, Alyssa Shaffer
**Design Director** Martin Elfers
**Senior Art Director** Pino Impastato
**Art Directors** Olga Jakim, Natali Suasnavas, Joseph Ulatowski
**Copy/Production** Patty Carroll, Angela Taormina
**Assistant Art Director** Jaclyn Loney
**Photo Editor** Keri Pruett
**Production Manager** Paul Rodina
**Production Assistant** Alyssa Swiderski
**Editorial Assistant** Tiana Schippa
**Sales & Marketing** Jeremy Nurnberg